BASKETBALL'S
TOUGHEST
CALLS

- BLOCK/CHARGE
- TRAVELING
- CONTACT/DISPLACEMENT

BY TODD KORTH

FROM *REFEREE* MAGAZINE & THE NATIONAL ASSOCIATION OF SPORTS OFFICIALS

Basketball's Toughest Calls:
Block/Charge, Traveling, Contact/Displacement

By Todd Korth, associate editor, *Referee*/NASO

Graphics and layout by Ross Bray, graphic designer, *Referee* magazine

Published by Referee Enterprises, Inc., and the National Association of Sports Officials.

Printed in the United States of America

ISBN-13: 978-1-58208-133-5

CONTENTS

INTRO

One of the thrills of basketball officiating that keeps us coming back for more is making a tough call and nailing it. Being in position, using solid, strong mechanics and knowing that you got that baby right. It's a sweet feeling no different than hitting a nice, straight drive off the tee.

But we all know that nailing a call in the span of a split-second is an ongoing challenge in any basketball game. Missed calls can and will surface like duffed shots in golf. Sometimes those missed calls cause us to lose sleep as we review a play in our heads over and over again into the night, wondering why we made a certain call or failed to make one. Was it poor positioning? Lack of rules knowledge? Weak mechanics? Admit it, we've all been there and really don't want to go back.

This book is for good basketball officials who are eager to make the transition to great in three areas where the calls are the most challenging in any game — block/charge, traveling and contact/displacement. How's that? Advice from leaders in basketball officiating who have offered their input on those tough calls. From the NBA's George Toliver to the NCAA's John Adams to the NFHS's Mary Struckhoff and many other supervisors and top, active officials, this book will teach you sound principles and give you a better understanding of what to look for when making a call. No matter where you are in your officiating career, the advice offered in this book can be applied to high school, college and even the professional levels. That will only lead you to better consistency while calling a game and a better night's sleep after each game!

We all are looking for ways to improve as officials. We review the rules, attend camps and clinics and talk over plays with each other as much as possible. The information offered in the following pages gives you another weapon to add to your arsenal.

I learned a ton by interviewing the experts and channeled their thoughts into three main chapters and many sub-chapters in a way that will help you learn, too. The advice offered by the experts is invaluable, so much so that we bolded their names everytime they offered their informative thoughts for easy, quick reference.

Read on, learn, improve your game and enjoy your season!

Todd Korth
Associate Editor
Referee magazine
National Association of Sports Officials

THE EXPERTS

JOHN ADAMS

NCAA national coordinator for men's basketball officials; former coordinator for men's basketball officials in the Horizon League (Division I), Great Lakes Valley (Division II) and Heartland Collegiate (Division III) conferences; former high school and collegiate basketball official.

ROGER BARR

Director of officials for the Iowa High School Athletic Association (IHSAA); officiated high school football, basketball and baseball for 30 years, including 23 state basketball tournaments (12 championship games).

JOE BORGIA

NBA vice president, referee operations; has also served as director of referee development and director of officiating programs and development; NBA referee from 1988-98; CBA referee from 1980-88; began his professional officiating career in 1978 at age 22 in the New York Pro-Am league.

PATTY BRODERICK

Coordinator of officials for Women's Basketball Officiating Consortium (includes Big Ten, Big 12, Conference USA, Horizon League, Summit, Great Lakes Valley, Mid-American, Missouri Valley conferences); former WNBA official and supervisor of officials; former NCAA women's basketball official; worked seven NCAA Final Four games.

ART HYLAND

Secretary-rules editor for the NCAA Men's
Basketball Rules Committee and coordinator of
men's basketball officials for the Big East
Conference; former associate commissioner for
football and basketball operations for the Eastern
College Athletic Conference; former assistant
coach for Princeton men's basketball.

DAVE LIBBEY

West Coast Conference coordinator of men's
basketball officials and former NCAA Division I
men's basketball referee for 30 years; officiated
eight NCAA Final Fours, including two national
championship games.

TOM LOPES

Executive director of the International
Association of Approved Basketball Officials
(IAABO) and supervisor of officials for the
Northeast Conference; former high school and
men's collegiate basketball official; worked 20
consecutive NCAA Division I tournaments and
three NCAA Final Fours; 1997 Naismith men's
college official of the year.

JOHN LOZANO

Instructional chair of California Basketball
Officials Association; current Division II and
Division III NCAA women's basketball official
and veteran high school official; California
Interscholastic Federation basketball state
interpreter.

MONTY MCCUTCHEN

Veteran NBA referee for 16 seasons; has officiated more than 1,000 regular season games and dozens of playoff games, including NBA Finals appearances the last two seasons; four seasons in CBA.

CURTIS SHAW

Former NCAA basketball, coordinator of men's officials for Conference USA, Big 12, Southland and Ohio Valley conferences and coordinator of women's basketball officials for the Ohio Valley and Atlantic Sun conferences.

MARY STRUCKHOFF

NCAA national coordinator of women's basketball officiating; NFHS assistant director; NFHS basketball and softball rules interpreter and editor; former NCAA Division I women's basketball official.

GEORGE TOLIVER

NBA director of D-League officials, has been a member of the NBA's Basketball Operations Department since 2004; NBA referee for 15 seasons, including the 1996 All Star Legends Game and the 1994 Japan Games in Yokohama.

DEBBIE WILLIAMSON

NCAA women's basketball secretary-rules editor; officiated NCAA women's basketball for five years and was selected to work three NCAA Division II women's basketball regional tournaments; former assistant coach at the NCAA Division I level for women's basketball and played on four Final Four teams at Louisiana Tech University.

CH1

CHAPTER

1

TRAVELING

What is the toughest call to make in basketball? Many will argue into the night that it is traveling because it happens so often during a typical game at any level. For as much as it is called, it is missed as much or more.

"The game has gotten lax in traveling over the last 10 to 15 years," said **Mary Struckhoff**, an NFHS assistant director, basketball rules interpreter, editor and NCAA national coordinator of women's basketball officiating. "I can find a DVD that Marcy (Weston, former NCAA women's basketball secretary-rules editor and national coordinator of women's basketball officials) and Hank (Nichols, former NCAA national coordinator of men's basketball officials) and Dick Schindler (former NFHS basketball rules editor) put together in 1994 and they were talking about the same things that we're talking about now, so I don't know that things have gotten a lot better."

A distinct advantage is gained when a player is permitted to travel and a distinct advantage is lost when traveling is incorrectly called by officials.

"You may have six to eight block/charge situations a game. You have hundreds of traveling possibilities in a game," said **Tom Lopes**, International Association of Approved Basketball Officials executive director, supervisor of officials for the Northeast Conference, and a self-proclaimed "travel nut." "Every time a player gets possession of the ball, it's a potential travel. Officials, number one, have to know which foot is the pivot foot or how the pivot foot is established. They must make sure as soon as the player receives the ball that they eye the foot that is going to be the pivot foot.

"I hate to agree with (former college coach and ESPN analyst) Bobby Knight, but I watched a video on YouTube that he had out about a year or two ago about traveling. He said it's the most miscalled violation by the officials, and it can have an impact on the game," **Lopes** said. "I watched a college game in person (last February), and the officials missed 11 travels that I recorded. And there may have been more. I think it's very difficult for the officials. Changing a pivot foot, repositioning or replanting, illegal moves in the post and illegal jump stops can add up to a lot of points over the course of a game."

In this chapter, we review all the rules that pertain to traveling situations and offer degrees of traveling, beginning with the toughest traveling calls to make to the very catchable violations. We also review situations in which a player is not traveling, but it is called anyway because it looks like the player is traveling. If you know what to look for, making the right call becomes a no-brainer.

"If we get a clear look at it, there's no excuse, but we often don't get a clear look at it and we're also worried about contact, so those are the excuses for missing travels," **Struckhoff** said. "I think over time we've used those excuses to an extreme and we've become complacent and say, 'Well, nobody else is calling it, so I'm not calling it even though I see it.'"

THE RULES

Traveling at the youth, high school and college levels is the same, though, at the NBA level the rules are different. No matter what the level, traveling is all about identifying the pivot foot after a player gains possession of the ball and concentrating, but that's easier said than done.

"I don't think as officials we're ever trained to pay attention to feet," says **John Adams**, NCAA national coordinator for men's basketball officials. "We're refereeing hands, we're refereeing shoulders, we're refereeing eyes, we're refereeing heads. The basketball itself attracts a lot of attention. And we're not kicking the ball. We're dribbling it or passing it or shooting it. I promise you, if you're allowed to kick it we probably would do better on traveling because you would spend more time looking at the feet."

Traveling, or running with the ball, is moving a foot or feet in any direction in excess of prescribed limits while holding the ball. The limits in NFHS and NCAA on foot movements are as follows:

A player who catches the ball with both feet on the floor may use either foot to pivot. When one foot is lifted, the other is the pivot foot.

A player, who catches the ball while moving or dribbling, may stop and establish a pivot foot.

"You have to know the pivot foot. That's top of the list," said **George Toliver**, director of NBA D-League officials and former NBA official. "First of all, when the person catches the ball you find the pivot foot. Then everything that goes on next is really in what I call pre-dribble travel mode. Obviously what the person does with his or her feet, if it's a split step, if it's a step and then a step forward, whatever he or she does that's legal or illegal prior to the release of the ball, that's what you then adjudicate. You have to get the catch, then find the pivot foot. Then it's really important that you referee from the floor up until he or she releases the ball. You have to train yourself to, even in an engaged match-up, to know what's happening with the feet in the release of the ball phase as the second component, which means refereeing from the floor up."

Here's where it gets a little trickier and demands discipline to locate the pivot foot as quickly as possible:

• If both feet are off the floor and the player lands simultaneously on both feet, either foot may be the pivot.

• If the player lands with one foot followed by the other, the first foot to touch is the pivot.

• If the player lands on one foot, he or she may jump off that foot and simultaneously land on both. Neither foot can be a pivot in that case.

• If one foot is on the floor it is the pivot when the other foot touches in a step. The player may jump off that foot and simultaneously land on both. Neither foot can be a pivot in this case.

• After coming to a stop and establishing a pivot foot, the pivot foot may be lifted, but not returned to the floor, before the ball is released on a pass or try for goal. If the player jumps, neither foot may be returned to the floor before the ball is released on a pass or try for goal. The pivot foot may not be lifted before the ball is released to start a dribble.

• After coming to a stop when neither foot can be a pivot, one or both feet may be lifted, but may not be returned to the floor before the ball is released on a pass or try for goal. Neither foot may be lifted before the ball is released to start a dribble.

"I was always trained from the day I started that as soon as you gain possession, and there was control and possession, immediately the second thing I look for after possession was the pivot foot," said **Curtis Shaw**, former NCAA basketball official who is coordinator of men's officials for Conference USA, Big 12, Southland and Ohio Valley conferences and also is coordinator of women's basketball officials for the Ohio Valley and Atlantic Sun conferences. "I've just always had it in my repertoire, one, did he have control? Two, which foot is the pivot foot? Whether it's in a fast-break situation; whether it's in a halfcourt receiving a pass situation; whether it's in a post-up, receiving a pass, no matter what."

• A player holding the ball may not touch the floor with a knee or any other part of the body other than hand or foot. After gaining control while on the floor and touching with other than his or her hand or foot, a player may not attempt to get up or stand.

Beginning a Dribble
Play: A1 receives a pass about 10 feet from team A's basket. A1 jumps to shoot but fears the shot may be blocked and lets go of the ball prior to returning to the floor. After returning to the floor, A1 (a) grabs the ball, or (b) dribbles it. Is this play legal? **Ruling:** It is a violation in both (a) and (b). Since A1 touched the ball again after releasing it, A1's initial release of the ball while in the air constituted the start of a dribble. A player may not begin a dribble after his or her pivot foot has left the floor. Since A1's pivot foot was off the ground when the dribble effectively began, a traveling violation results. Had A1 not touched the ball after returning to the floor, the play would be legal.

Illegal Dribble?
Play: A1 is dribbling in team A's frontcourt and ends the dribble. While under defensive pressure from B2, A1 pivots away from B2, but while holding the ball with both hands, A1 loses his or her balance and the ball touches the floor while still in A1's hands. Has a violation occurred? **Ruling:** It is not a dribble when a player is holding the ball and touches it to the floor. A dribble can only be started by pushing, throwing, tapping or batting the ball to the floor. Therefore, A1 has not dribbled a second time, and no double dribble violation has occurred.

Power Dribble
Play: A1 passes the ball into post player, A5. A5 pivots toward the basket, pushes the ball to the floor with both hands simultaneously in a "power dribble" movement, catches the ball with both hands and shoots it. Is this power dribble illegal since it was started with both hands simultaneously? **Ruling 3:** No, this is a legal play. A dribble may be started by pushing, throwing, tapping or batting the ball to the floor. While it is true that a dribble ends when the dribble touches the ball with both hands simultaneously, a dribble can be started with either one or both hands.

THE PENALTY

When traveling occurs, the ball is dead when the violation occurs and is awarded to the opponents for a throw-in from the designated out-of-bounds spot nearest the violation.

LOCATE THE PIVOT

When a player holds the ball and is in contact with the floor, that player establishes a pivot foot. It will be the first one that touches the ground or, if they're both contacting the floor as control is established, the player establishes the pivot foot by taking a step with the other.

"If you don't have it, don't guess," said **Dave Libbey**, West Coast Conference coordinator of men's basketball officials and an NCAA Division I referee for 30-plus years. "Just because it looked funny or looked like something else, that doesn't mean it's traveling."

At slow motion or maybe even walking speed, locating the pivot foot is not too tough a task. However, consider a fast break with the players moving full speed. You have to figure out when the ball was caught, where the feet were when it was caught, what happened with the feet while the ball was in the hands of the player and when the ball was released on either a try, pass or dribble. All that must be done while you are also trying to decide if the defensive player is fouling or establishing position for the block/charge call that might be coming.

TRAIL OR CENTER CAN HELP

The task of the lead official in halfcourt isn't easy when wide bodies shove for position on rebounds or entry passes and post players exchange arm bars and strategically extended knees. Trying to observe all of that and watch the player's feet is nearly impossible.

"The officials are concerned more with the contact as opposed to the travel," **Lopes** said. "It just appears that way to me. But in the three-person crew and two person crew, everybody has to be aware of a possible travel situation. I think the hardest travel calls are in the post."

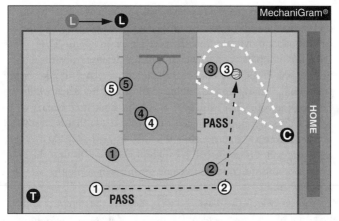

The center and trail official in three-person crews can assist with determining a legal drop step and a traveling double pivot.

That's where the center and trail official in three-person crew and the trail in two-person crews can assist with determining a legal drop step and a traveling double pivot.

"I would say more often than not, that is a tough call for the lead because when the ball comes into the post, you've got an arm in the back and you've got another guy bumping him, which official has the easiest view of the pivot?" said **Libbey**. "It's the center or the trail, absolutely.

"If the ball is on the lead side, it's the trail who picks up the pivot. If I'm the lead and I start looking down at that foot, trying to find the (pivot), I'm going to miss the shove in the back or the hold or the (arm) hook that the offensive guy is doing," **Libbey** said. "When that ball comes down to the low post, the primary is going to be that trail and when it turns away from the lead across the key to the center, we always say, 'When it goes away, stay away from the lead.' That goes with fouls and everything else. So when the ball goes to the center, the lead will see that step or jump stop. It used to be that everything comes from the lead. Not necessarily; good help will come from that trail who finds the pivot foot."

REFEREE THE DEFENSE AND THE PIVOT

A player dribbling the ball has as much freedom of movement as skill and the relevant lines on the floor permit. A player holding the ball is much more limited and the defense's job is to make that individual regret that predicament. If the player has already picked up the dribble and established a pivot foot, the defender can probably move with the offensive player and control the direction of a pass or shot, which is to the defense's advantage. So, the first illegal way out is for the offensive player to take extra steps while picking up the dribble or to extend the reach while holding the ball. That extra footwork is most likely to occur when a defender pops out against the dribbler, so that is another excellent time to catch traveling. First, look for the attacker to catch the ball. Once the ball is caught, look down to find the pivot foot and watch for it to come down again while the attacker still has the ball. If it does, call traveling.

You can watch the player holding the ball, the defender and be aware of the movement of the pivot foot if you are far enough away. If you are too close, it's difficult to notice a player's feet and then you are forced to rely on one of your partners to call the travel for you if it happens.

Once you learn to watch the pivot foot, you begin to get better at anticipating when a travel is coming — not anticipating the call, but anticipating when it might happen. At the high school level, there tends to be many more "one-footed" basketball players than in the colleges or pros. That is, there are players who are much more comfortable driving off of one foot over the other. In a practical sense, what that means is that a player is likely to try to establish one pivot foot rather than the other under pressure — and gets in trouble when he or she can't. Often, a right-handed player will try to establish a right-footed pivot so that he or she can do a crossover step and drive to the right quickly while shielding the ball. If the player tries to set a left-foot pivot and then cross over and drive left instead, that player will try to pull the right foot through and, to do it quickly enough, shuffle his or her pivot foot. If you keep track of the pivot foot, the play calls itself.

Another situation in which watching the pivot foot makes the call easier occurs on those long drives down the lane. A dribbler either picks up the dribble and kind of hopscotches past defenders or receives a feed in traffic and looks for a crease to the hoop without putting the ball down while making a spin move. If you try to take a picture of the whole play and then ask yourself, "Was that two steps (or four, or many more)?" you will probably react too late. The reality is that, in either of those cases, the player is going to try to catch the ball (either picking up his or her dribble or taking the pass) with both feet off the floor because he or she needs all the steps possible to make it to the hole.

"If you're out of position, you're not going to be able to see those things," says **John Lozano,** instructional chair of the California Basketball Officials Association and veteran high school and women's college official. "We try to say that you need to correct the big problem first, then start working on the smaller gray areas. If you're not in good position, it makes it difficult to pick up the easy stuff. Once we get the easy stuff, then we start discussing the spin move, and are they dragging their pivot foot, or whether a jump stop is right or not."

If the dribbler can protract catching the ball after the dribble, that player can gain an unfair advantage. A double-dribble violation makes no distinction between touching the ball twice between bounces and touching the ball twice while catching it after bouncing it. So, if the attacker taps the ball from one hand to the other while catching it, or lets it spin in the hand while running with it, that's traveling. He or she might try to do that to squeeze between two defenders who have established a legal guarding position.

Art Hyland, NCAA Men's Basketball Rules Committee secretary-rules editor and supervisor of men's basketball officials for the Big East Conference, says many officials blur the interval between catching the ball while airborne and landing to try to get extra steps. In either scenario, officials get fooled because they try to see the catch and see the pivot foot being established as a combined event — it's too much information to process at once. The feet don't matter until the ball is caught: Look from the catch to the pivot foot and, if it comes down again, no amount of graceful pirouetting can disguise the travel.

Now, what if the offensive player receives the ball, establishes a pivot foot and still has the option to dribble? A very high percentage of the time, the attacker will have a "favorite" pivot foot because his or her opposite hand is the favorite dribbling or shooting hand, so defenders are taught to deny any movement in that favored direction. When the defender denies that preferred route, you would be amazed at how often the attacker merely lifts the pivot foot to set off away from the pressure rather than taking a crossover step first. That is traveling.

Especially at the high school level, if guards are weaker off of one pivot foot than the other, then a post player is downright clumsy. A typical move is to roll into position with his or her back to the basket, receive a pass from the perimeter and then turn and face up, establishing a pivot foot in the process. Watch then for that player to lift the pivot foot as part of the next movement. Watch the post players during the warmups and they'll already be making that error. Also watch for a post player to step from one pivot foot onto another as part of making a turnaround jumper in the paint: To the player it's a safe, but it's an illegal substitute for putting the ball on the floor in traffic.

"If an official rules by movement of a player he or she will be lucky to get 50 percent of the traveling calls correct," said **Roger Barr**, director of officials for the Iowa High School Athletic Association. "The crossover/step-through move is a perfect example of how important it is to identify the pivot foot, mainly used in the post area. Perfectly legal in some cases and in others, players totally switch pivot feet."

Being able to consistently get traveling calls right does seem to separate the wheat from the chaff. But practice doesn't make perfect in getting better at making those calls if we don't apply a technique to breaking the play down as we observe it.

"I think a consistency really is important for the game," **Lopes** said. "I think you need to get the first walk, but I think you need to get almost every walk."

RULES ARE DIFFERENT IN NBA

When LeBron James drives to the basket and takes three steps en route to an acrobatic slam dunk, many, including amateur officials, will cry for traveling, even though by NBA rules, it is perfectly legal.

Traveling in the NBA is slightly different than in NFHS and NCAA. An NBA player is allowed two steps *after* his pivot foot is lifted upon gathering the ball, according to the NBA rulebook. "Some players are learning and purposely picking their dribble up as soon as the ball comes off the floor," said **Joe Borgia**, NBA vice president of referee operations. "So a player can almost go three full steps because he gets two steps after (picking up the dribble).

"These guys are some unbelievable athletes," Borgia said. "They've got some long legs and can go real far in two legal steps."

Also, it is not traveling in the NBA if a player falls to the ground with possession of the ball. In NFHS and NCAA it is traveling when that occurs. But it is traveling in the NBA if a player catches his own missed shot after it misses the rim and before it hits the floor. In NFHS and NCAA, it is legal for a player to catch his or her missed shot as long as it is unintentional.

THE BIG THREE

There are many different forms of traveling, but **Hyland**, who says he has been watching video of basketball games "for 100 years," believes that three common traveling violations occur during a game more than any other.

"One is in the post," Hyland said. "When post players initially get the ball they tend to travel a lot. Not so much when they're making their move, but when they initially get the ball. We ask our outside officials to help with that. If you look at the lead official when the post player gets the ball, he's looking up top where the ball is. That's where fouls occur and he's really not looking at the feet as much as he is where the ball is. His peripheral vision isn't nearly as good as when you're further away. So we ask the outside officials to help on post play with traveling.

"Secondly, when people are moving quickly, especially big players, are moving in transition quickly and are passed the ball, they don't know how to stop," **Hyland** said. "You have to watch when a pass is made in quick transition, watch what they do because as you know when a player comes down on one foot, that becomes his pivot foot, so he can only make one other step. A lot of times they just aren't good enough to be able to stop. A lot of kids have gone to the two-footed jump stop, which enables them to stop more quickly, but you need to at least be aware in your mind when kids are in transition, especially big players, they aren't as good at stopping with the ball as a guard might be.

"Then the third is a lot of offensive sets end up with a player getting the ball at the top of the key," **Hyland** said. "Look at the number of shots that are taken there. When screens are set and all that kind of stuff, and a player all of a sudden is coming off a little curl and he gets the ball, then stops and starts again, a lot of times you get a change in the pivot foot. That's another area where you really need to identify the pivot foot when he catches the ball so you know what he can do with his other foot and what he can't do. If we can get most of the travels correct on those three types of plays, then I think we're doing OK.

BUNNY HOP TO A VIOLATION

Most players need a jump shot, especially from three-point range, right? On well-coached teams, the perimeter shooters are taught to catch a feed while airborne. That way, they can land on two feet and use the momentum they build while stepping legally off of one foot to put power into the shot. Alternatively, they'll already have a pivot foot established as they catch the pass and use their turn to the basket on that pivot foot to build momentum.

On the other teams, you'll see them catch the ball flat-footed and then bunny hop onto both feet again to shoot, which is traveling. Visually, it's very subtle but technically it's lifting and replanting the pivot foot.

"It's kind of a double-edged sword because I do think that sometimes our officials like to take the path of least resistance and they think that nobody's guarding this kid and she just has a habitual move that is illegal, but the nearest defender is 20 feet away, so who cares?" said **Struckhoff**. "Still, it's illegal. Then we get the regular excuses of 'there was body contact and bodies moving and I didn't see it.'"

Remember to reward legal coaching and instruction.

SPIN MOVE

Of all the different ways to commit a traveling violation, the spin move is perhaps the toughest to nail down because it happens so quickly. Yet, in most cases, when the video of the play is slowed down, it is clearly a traveling violation. Locating and then keeping an eye on the pivot foot as a ballhandler/dribbler quickly makes a spin toward the basket is a daunting task.

A spin move is typically utilized by the dribbler to create separation from his or her defender and close the distance to the basket. It is an exciting and athletic move; however, the rules regarding traveling must still be followed, yet officials often look the other way.

"I'm going to say it's an illegal move, and I've heard it referenced that way and I agree with it because they're lifting the pivot foot," says **Lozano**. "They have the pivot foot down on the floor, they lift it and put it back down with possession of the ball, and that's a travel. This is an example where the game has evolved with a lot of speed and motion, and players have picked up this move that they've seen it on the higher level. But because of that I think you see it a lot more in college and you see it in high school.

"When I've seen our officials working high school, I really find that they just are not calling it, and they need to," **Lozano** said. "I think we just need to do a consistent job of changing our mind-set and realizing that it is illegal and being able to see it, we don't want to just call it automatically, but when you see it you need to quickly know where that pivot foot is and realize it's being lifted, put back down and call a travel."

It also is another area in which the trail or center officials in three-person crews are more likely to see the traveling violation.

When the player gathers the ball — usually with two hands — by rule, he or she has ended the dribble and establishes a pivot foot. That pivot foot may be lifted but it must not be returned to the playing court before the ball is released on a pass or try for goal. Many players at all levels are performing that move illegally when they gather the ball and establish a pivot foot, spin on the other foot and then return the pivot foot to the court as a "plant" foot before releasing the ball on a pass or try for goal. That is likely done to change the player's momentum from horizontal to vertical and propel him or her upward for a jump shot. It happens fast and so fast that it is often missed by officials, but once that pivot foot is returned to the court without releasing the ball, a traveling violation has occurred.

Whether the move is made by a post player or a guard making a drive to the lane area, in many cases the spin move is a traveling violation.

"You know the drop step that all coaches teach pivot players?" asked **Hyland**. "If you can picture a player with his back to the basket and I have the ball in my hand, and I drop step with my right foot, now I turn and I put my other foot down on the floor before I shoot, that's a travel. When I drop step with my right foot, that means my left foot is my pivot foot. When I now lift that pivot foot and put it down on the floor again, it's a travel. That means that all the drop steps, unless there's some type of a dribble utilized with it, all the drop steps are technically travels.

"The spin move that the guards use in transition, it's the same move, just going 100 times faster," **Hyland** said. "They come and they set their right foot as their pivot foot, they drop, they spin on their left foot, and put their right foot down before they shoot. Travel."

While most officials will agree that spin moves are generally illegal, they are not always called and rarely do players and coaches complain that they are traveling violations. The excitement factor of the athletic move is likely part and sometimes most of the reason for allowing the play to stand.

"Unless the basketball world is willing to address the drop step and the spin move, which are the same thing, and say from here on it's going to be called a travel, otherwise you'll create a furor," **Hyland** said. "They're great plays that kids make, and people love them. Are we going to interrupt the game that much? I don't know. But you and I both know that when you slow the tape down it's a travel."

JUMP STOP

The "standard" jump stop is when a dribbler ending the dribble or a player catching a pass with both feet off the floor, and landing simultaneously on both feet, has not established a pivot foot and can now choose either as the pivot. From that position, it's tough to pass, but it's easier and legal to jump and shoot, which will often happen all in the same motion when picking up a dribble. To tell a legal jump stop from a travel, however, you still must look from the catch to the feet.

After that, jump stops get a little more difficult. Consider the following situations.

REFEREE CASEPLAY

Landing Simultaneously on Both Feet
Play: With one foot on the floor, A1 (a) catches a pass, or (b) ends a dribble, jumps off that foot and lands simultaneously on both feet. Or with both feet off the floor, A1 (a) catches a pass, or (b) ends a dribble, lands on one foot, jumps off that foot and lands simultaneously on both feet.
Ruling: Both situations are legal jump stops. However, unlike the standard jump stop, the player cannot pivot on either foot from that point. Lifting either foot and returning it to the floor before the ball is released on a try for goal or pass is a traveling violation. Lifting either foot before releasing the ball to start a dribble is also a traveling violation. Note that on a dribble following a "no pivot" jump stop, the foot does not have to return to the floor before release to violate — simply lifting it before release is enough for a whistle.

The different types of jump stops described all have one key element in common — the simultaneous touching of both feet ending the jump stop.

"It happens quickly, no doubt, but if we are in doubt, we typically let it go," said Struckhoff. "Where I think we've fudged a little bit is on the simultaneous landing on the two feet. I think we've gotten a little complacent and the line in the sand has moved a bit. They're coming one-two instead of down together. We're letting that go."

Lifts a Foot After Landing Simultaneously on Both Feet

Play: A3 catches the ball while one foot is on the floor and the other is off the floor. A3 jumps off that foot and lands on both feet simultaneously. A3 then (a) lifts a foot and starts a dribble, (b) lifts a foot and shoots the ball, (c) lifts a foot and passes the ball, or (d) takes a step with either foot, then shoots the ball. **Ruling:** In (a), it is a traveling violation as A3 does not have a pivot foot, and neither foot can be lifted before starting a dribble. In (b) and (c), the play is legal as A3, when having no pivot foot, can shoot or pass the ball after lifting a foot but before it returns to the floor. In (d), it is a traveling violation as A3 has no pivot foot. A3's foot was lifted and returned to the floor before shooting the ball.

Pivot Foot Touches Floor Twice

Play: A3, moving without the ball, comes off a screen. With neither foot on the floor, A3 catches a pass from A2. A3's right foot touches the floor, followed by the left foot. A3 then pivots off the left foot, swinging the right foot around to square up to the basket. **Ruling:** In NFHS and NCAA, A3 has traveled. The first foot that touched the court, the right foot, is automatically the pivot foot because A3's feet did not land simultaneously. Lifting the right foot and placing it back on the floor is a violation, albeit a difficult one to recognize.

Watch closely and you will see the maneuver happen often without a call, particularly with a player moving away from the basket. The "extra" step doesn't look wrong. Often, the offensive player gains no discernable advantage and calling the violation might be considered a "game stopper." However, if the extra step helps A3 create enough space from a pressuring defender to get a shot off or open a passing lane, the violation should be called.

Step After Jump Stop

Play: A5 drives toward the free-throw line, ends the dribble with one foot on the floor, jumps off that foot and lands with both feet simultaneously to the floor. Meanwhile, A4 cuts toward the basket. A5 takes one step toward A4 and makes a perfect bounce pass for the layup. **Ruling:** The jump stop does not permit either foot to be the pivot. While stepping into a bounce pass is textbook execution, in that case it is also traveling.

Differentiating between a legal jump stop and traveling is one of the more difficult calls to make.

"You've got to understand that if you go off one foot and land on two, you can't pivot," Libbey said. "There are little keys to it. The key is: How far is that jump stop? Guys come up the court and as they're dribbling, they come off one foot and land on two and then stop their dribble, there's a pivot on that. It's when you stop your dribble, go off one foot and land on two feet. The distance has a lot to do with it. They'll go five, six feet. Once that happens, now you're locked in. You can only jump up or pass the ball."

DON'T GUESS ON TRAVELING

Officials sometimes stop a game for a traveling violation that simply isn't there, which only frustrates other officials, players and coaches. The player may have moved his or her feet oddly, making his or her actions look funny. That, combined with coaches, players and fans howling for traveling doesn't make it right to call a traveling violation.

"You can't call it because it looks funny or it doesn't look right," said **Libbey**. "So many people go, 'That didn't look right, it had to be traveling.' You can't guess on it. I even tell my guys, 'If we're going to miss one, let's miss one by not calling one that's there instead of calling one that's not there and taking away a good play from somebody. These kids are strong, they've got crossovers, they've got all these different moves, so you've really got to find the pivot foot to begin with. That's when you learn the mechanics of it and learn what you should be doing. The biggest thing is don't guess and don't call something because it looked a little strange, it looked a little funny. You've got to be 100 percent on traveling. You really have to do that otherwise it will screw up the game by calling a good move.

"We do a lot of tape work, a tremendous amount," **Libbey** said. "Our guys look at DVDs after the game, break it down. Before the game, we have plays that we look at and we really emphasize that. In our pregame and we talk about it. Don't guess."

Hyland says that officials make two kinds of errors in games — error of commission and error of omission. That is particularly true with traveling violations.

"If a player travels and the official doesn't call the travel, now the supervisor looks at the tape and says, 'Hey Joe, that was a travel; you should've called it.' That's a mistake," said **Hyland**, explaining error of omission. "But what has happened in the game? Other than the offensive player having a slight advantage because he traveled and got away with it, the players still play on. There's been no interruption in the game and the players are still playing hard. They don't even know that there should've been a travel.

"On the other hand, an error of commission, let's say that you call a travel and we look back at the tape and there was no travel," **Hyland** said. "What have you done now? Number one, you've stopped the game. Number two, you've taken the ball away from team A, and that's a turnover. That in my mind is a worse mistake than the error of omission. You've given the ball to the other team, or if it was a shooting foul and there was no foul, you've given the team two points that they shouldn't have gotten. Those mistakes in my mind are far worse than the errors of omission.

"What I've tried to do is make sure the official understands that when you blow your whistle you must be right. Your mistakes are going to be when you don't blow your whistle," **Hyland** said.

Women, whether it is in high school or college, make legal moves in regard to body movement and use of the non-pivot foot that may not always be similar to moves made by men. So it is imperative for women's basketball officials not to penalize players just because a move looks unusual.

"There was a time, even when I was coaching 25 years ago, that every time a female player head-faked, they would call a travel, and it wasn't," said **Debbie Williamson**, secretary-rules editor of NCAA women's basketball. "There's been a consistent theme for a long time in the women's game that they can make some legal moves that may not look like the men, but officials have to determine first of all are they legal, and if they are legal, don't penalize it.

"The role of the rules committee is to look at rules that we currently have, and the rule hasn't changed in who knows how long, so we're not changing the rule," **Williamson** said. "We just feel like if we post video clips of what is legal and what is illegal; if we go over the rule and teach people what is legal and illegal; then all of us, everybody in the game, officials, coaches, players, can learn what they can do and what they can't do, which will improve consistency. The cry continued through last year, so the committee again kept it as a point of emphasis for the third year in a row."

JABBING WITH NON-PIVOT FOOT

How many times have you seen or even called traveling on a post player who makes a few jab steps with his or her non-pivot foot while trying to fake out a defender in an effort to get off a shot? Calling a violation on a player who has not committed a traveling violation happens frequently at all levels and mainly because the official did not correctly locate his or her pivot foot.

"He can step all he wants as long as he's not moving that pivot foot," **Libbey** said. "Say his left is his pivot and he takes a small step with his right, then a big step with his right, the crowd goes crazy because they think he's walking. But he's never moved his pivot foot. If you don't know which one is his pivot foot, you're going to make a bad call."

PIVOT FOOT IS OFF FLOOR

A player with the ball can lift his or her pivot foot off the floor, but it cannot touch the floor again while that player is still in possession of the ball. Simple right? But many coaches, some players and most fans will go nuts when a player, especially on the perimeter, takes a step with his or her non-pivot foot while lifting his or her pivot before making a pass to taking a shot. They will exclaim, "You can't lift your pivot foot. That's traveling!" If that's the case, it would be difficult to make a layup because a player's pivot foot often leaves the ground as he or she steps onto his or her jumping leg to execute the shot. The pivot foot leaves the ground but doesn't return to the ground until the ball is released.

Similarly, if a player passes the ball, he or she is allowed to lift the pivot foot and make the pass off the other foot because it's part of the normal motion of releasing the ball, which the traveling rule is intended to permit. In those two cases, the traveling rule does kick in again if the player decides to bail out of the shooting or passing action. Sometimes that does permit the rather awkward looking pose, seen in many middle school games, of a player balancing interminably on one foot after trying to pass the ball, while parents yell for a violation. Sorry folks, that's legal.

PLAYER SLIDES ON FLOOR WITH BALL

A loose ball is rolling down the floor. A guard runs after the ball at full speed and dives for the ball. After securing the ball on the floor, the player's momentum causes him or her to (a) slide on his or her stomach before coming to a stop, (b) slide on his or her back before coming to a stop, or (c) roll over several times before coming to a stop. After coming to a stop, the guard passes the ball to a team. Has a violation occurred in any of the three situations? No. It is legal for a player's momentum to cause the player to slide or roll after gaining possession of the basketball while on the floor. Yet, it is at that point when many officials succumb to the shouts from others in the gym or arena to call traveling, which is the last thing an official should do in any of those situations. Why penalize a player who made a hustling, physical play to secure the ball, only to take it away from him or her with a tweet of the whistle?

Once a player's momentum is no longer causing him or her to slide or roll, and that player has come to a complete stop, he or she may not roll over or stand up without violating unless he or she had first started a dribble while on the floor. That means that the player could technically start dribbling the ball and get up off the ground simultaneously and not be called for traveling. That player, if flat on his or her back, also can sit up and either shoot the ball or pass it to a teammate. However, the player cannot put the ball on the floor, quickly stand up and be the first to touch it. That's traveling.

If a player secures control of the ball while both knees are in contact with the floor, he or she is allowed to pass to a teammate, try for a goal or call a timeout. He or she also can start dribbling the ball and rise to his or her feet. However, that player cannot lift one knee off the ground, put that foot on the floor and raise the remaining knee off the ground in an effort to get up. In that case, it's traveling.

Rising From Knees

Play: A1 secures control of the ball while both knees are in contact with the floor. A1 (a) lifts one knee off the ground, puts that foot on the floor and raises the remaining knee off the ground in an effort to get up, (b) passes to a teammate, tries for a goal or calls timeout, or (c) starts dribbling the ball and raises to his or her feet. Has A1 committed a violation? **Ruling:** A1 has committed a traveling violation in (a). Any attempt by A1 to stand up while holding the ball is traveling. A1 traveled the instant A1's knee was raised off the ground. In (b) and (c), no violation has occurred. All of A1's actions are legal.

PLAYER MUFFS BALL

One of the fundamentals to remember about traveling is that it is not possible for a player to travel during a dribble. With that in mind, let's say that B4 grabs the rebound after a missed team A field goal attempt and spots B5 streaking toward the basket. B4 throws the long pass to B5, who muffs the ball several times while running before securing it. B5 takes several steps between the time the ball was first touched and when the ball was finally controlled. Should a traveling violation be called?

Although the play looks very awkward, and team A's coach and most fans may voice their disapproval, no violation has occurred. As long as B5's bobbling of the basketball is truly incidental during the attempt to control it, traveling should not be called. In order for traveling to occur, the player must hold the ball prior to moving a foot or feet in excess of the limits described in the traveling rule. Since B5 was not holding the ball while muffing it during the attempted catch, a traveling violation hasn't occurred.

CATCH YOUR OWN PASS

Yet another example of a play where most fans, many coaches and some players will scream for a traveling violation, when in reality it isn't, is when a player shoots, often in the lane area, and catches his or her own shot after it falls well short of hitting the rim.

For example, A1 attempts a try for goal. The try is well short of the rim. A1 follows the shot, catches the ball, makes another attempt and is successful. Is A1's action legal? Has A1 traveled? If in the official's mind, A1's first attempt was a legitimate attempt for a goal that was just extremely short, A1's actions are legal. Score two points for A1. If the official feels A1's actions were not sincere in trying for a goal, traveling should be called.

TRAVELING CHECKLIST

☑ Identify the pivot foot after a player gains possession of the ball.

☑ The center or trail official in three-person crews can assist with determining a legal drop step and a traveling double pivot.

☑ Referee the defense and the pivot. Look for extra footwork to occur when a defender pops out against the dribbler.

☑ Three popular kinds of traveling violations include bunny hops, spin moves and jump stops. A bunny hop can be very subtle just and a spin move very quick. Know what players can and cannot do in each situation.

☑ Don't guess on traveling. Don't make a call because something doesn't look right. Jabbing with the non-pivot foot, lifting a pivot foot off the floor, sliding on the floor with the ball or a muffed ball may look like weird but it's not traveling.

☑ NBA rules on traveling are slightly different than in NFHS and NCAA.

CHAPTER 2

BLOCK/CHARGE

Sometimes it is as if a block/charge play happens in slow motion. The dribbler is making his or her way quickly on a drive to the basket and you see a defender out of the corner of your eye slide into position a few feet from the basket in an attempt to draw the charge. Then, boom! The play explodes, bodies are flying to the floor and it's up to you to make a decision. So much for the slow motion. Block? Charge? Whaddya gonna decide? Were you watching the defender? Was he or she stepping into position on time? Too late? Facing the dribbler? Did the dribbler try to go around the defender with slight contact or did he or she go through the defender on the way to the basket?

There are many elements of a play to observe in next to no time in a block/charge situation. Sometimes the calls are easy and sometimes it's literally a call that barely teeters one way or the other on the fine line of block/charge.

"The block/charge play always involves knowing if the defender was in legal guarding position before the contact occurred," says **John Adams**, NCAA national coordinator for men's basketball officials. "The adage, 'referee the defense,' is never more important than it is for this play. Have a patient whistle, referee the defense, and you will dramatically increase your chances to get this play right."

This chapter breaks down blocking and charging fouls, including caseplays of various situations, plus a review of mechanics for two-person and three-person crews to help you get the call right. A number of high-ranking supervisors and officials throughout the country have chimed in with their opinion on the best way to observe and decide on whether it's a block or a charge when that type of play explodes on you.

BLOCKING FOUL RULES

In NFHS and NCAA, blocking is illegal personal contact which impedes the progress of an opponent with or without the ball and shall be penalized, according to the rules.

• To establish an initial legal guarding position on a player with the ball, the guard shall have both feet touching the playing court and his or her torso must be facing the opponent. When the opponent with the ball is airborne, the guard shall have attained legal position before the opponent left the playing court.

• A player may hold his or her hands and arms in front of his or her face or body for protection and to absorb force from an imminent charge by an opponent in an attempt to draw a player control foul. Defenders also can move to maintain a legal guarding position, either sideways or backwards. But a player shall not hold, push, trip or impede the progress of an opponent by extending his or her arm(s), shoulder(s), hip(s) or knee(s) or by bending his or her own body into other than a normal position while guarding an opponent.

• Under all codes, when a dribbler, without contact, sufficiently passes an opponent to have his or her head and shoulders in advance of that opponent, the greater responsibility for that subsequent contact is on the opponent.

"It's not easy," said NFHS Assistant Director **Mary Struckhoff**, who serves as NFHS basketball rules interpreter and editor, plus is NCAA national coordinator of women's basketball officiating. "There are a lot of factors. Then you have the rules side of it depending what rule code you are in. If you are officiating men's collegiate, you can't be under the basket. If you're officiating women's collegiate or high school, you can be. It's about refereeing the defense. It's about getting two feet down and facing the opponent."

Roger Barr, director of officials for the Iowa High School Athletic Association, urges officials to ask themselves a simple question before making a block/charge call: "What did the defensive player do wrong? Once a defensive player has established a legal guarding position, his or her entire body has established a legal guarding position. With that said, if an offensive player makes contact with the defensive player, it doesn't make any difference what part of the defensive player's body the contact occurred on, the foul should be charged to the offense," **Barr** said.

Bottom line, if there is contact aside from anything close to incidental, make a call. Sounds simple, but **Adams** is far from convinced that officials are consistently ruling one way or the other in a block/charge situation. At least at the NCAA men's level, he said he has seen too many no-calls in recent seasons.

"It was an old-school of thought that one of your options on block/charge plays to the basket was a no-call," said **Adams**. "We actually had it in the rulebook two years ago and that has since been removed. So we are kind of retraining or changing the culture away from the idea that a no-call is an acceptable outcome. It's just going to take a little more time than I want to see it take.

"With the exception of pure incidental contact, when you have a crash at the basket, it's either a block or a charge."

NCAA MEN'S SECONDARY DEFENDER

NCAA men's basketball included in its 2010 and 2011 rulebook the definition of a secondary defender, "a teammate who has helped a primary defender after that player has been beaten by an opponent because he failed to establish or maintain a legal guarding position." To discourage a secondary defensive player from attaining initial guarding position under the basket with the sole purpose of drawing a charge rather than making a legitimate attempt to play the offensive player, the NCAA rules committee passed a rule prior to the 2009-10 season that calls for such an action to be called a block on the defensive player. So, if a portion of the defender's body is under the basket ring, it is a block. "Under the basket" is defined as from the front of the side of the ring to the front of the backboard. The player is considered under the basket when any part of either foot is in that area. That rule change does not discourage team defense in that the "help" by the secondary defensive player may be established anywhere on the playing court other than under the basket.

In establishing a position in any multiple-defender, fast-break situation, a player shall not establish initial legal guarding position under the basket, or a blocking foul will be called.

Adams says that, for the most part, the restricted area has helped create more balance between the offense and defense, and has "served as a deterrent for players positioning themselves under the basket soley to take a charge."

With that in mind, the NCAA will be experimenting in men's basketball during the 2010 preseason NIT and multi-team tournaments the use of an arc drawn on the floor two feet from the center of the basket. In the NBA, the arc is four feet from the center of the basket.

"Our rule is predicated on balance between offense and defense," **Adams** said. "If you put that arc four feet from the center of the basket like the NBA has it, I think you change the balance between offense and defense. I think you tip the balance in favor of the offense."

NCAA women have no imaginary ring under the basket that officials must consider when making a block/charge call.

"In my opinion that's the toughest call — the secondary defender sliding down," said **Patty Broderick**, coordinator of the Women's Basketball Officiating Consortium, which includes seven Division I conferences and one Division II conference, and a former NCAA and WNBA official. "Then obviously you've got to have help from the back side and the off officials who are not on the ball to make sure that they did get there before that offensive player left the floor. That is a tough play. I'm not a proponent of the arc. I just think it creates more work for the officials. You've got all kinds of barriers you've got to deal with: Was it a secondary defender; were her feet on the arc and so on.

"I swear to goodness, that it is a 50/50 play," **Broderick** said. "The good thing is you got a whistle on the darn play, and if it's a block, fine; if it's a charge, that's fine, too. They're just that close sometimes."

Like college and pro officials, high school officials must beware of secondary defenders as well. Secondary defenders are becoming more prevalent throughout the various levels of basketball in recent years. In most cases, the lead official will be picking up the secondary defender.

"A three-person crew helps, but when we've got a drive coming from the outside, the primary official is going to be the center or the trail, so the lead really has to pick up that secondary defender moving," said **Struckhoff**. "The lead is going to have the best look at (the secondary defender). What complicates it is we have the primary official, who has the play from the beginning and it's moving to the basket and now you've got the secondary defender being picked up by a different official and that's where we get 'blarges' (one official calls a blocking foul and one official calls a player control foul). It's about communication and it's about ego. Who saw what?

"I do think that at the women's collegiate level, our folks have done a pretty good job of recognizing who's got the secondary defender and then releasing, if you are the primary official on the play. If not, there has to be good communication for when two officials have different signals and what to do. It's the coming together and the good communication of who had what.

"Part of problem in high school games is that they are often officiated by two-person crews, so it might complicate it more," **Struckhoff** said. "In those situations, the lead can still help depending on what side of floor he or she is coming from."

Contact Underneath the Basket

Play: A1 drives toward the basket and beats his or her defender, B2, near the basket. A secondary defender, B3, moves to a position directly underneath the basket. B3 has both feet on the floor and is facing A1 prior to A1 leaving the floor for a shot attempt. A1's momentum causes the player to crash into B3 after A1 has released the try for goal, but prior to A1 returning to the floor. A1's try goes in. Has a foul occurred? Shall the basket count? **Ruling:** In NFHS and NCAA women, legal guarding position can be obtained anywhere on the basketball court. Therefore, B3's guarding position is legal and a player-control foul shall be called on A1 since A1 was an airborne shooter. A1's basket shall not count and team B shall receive a throw-in. In NCAA men, a secondary defender must establish guarding position outside the area from the front to the rim to the front of the backboard. Therefore, B3, who is a secondary defender, is not in legal guarding position. B3 shall be charged with a blocking foul. A1's goal shall count, and A1 shall receive one free throw for being fouled on a successful try.

"The rules are different," said Dave Libbey, West Coast Conference coordinator of men's basketball officials and an NCAA Division I referee for 30-plus years. "We're seeing more and more under the basket. The game is better off because we're calling more blocks on secondary defenders, guys who are sliding in there and jumping in there.

"There's an old analogy and I called it that way, too: If you got hit in the chest, it's a charge. Well, it's not that way with a secondary defender. They've got to be there, as well as where they are on the floor and which direction they are coming from."

TO AND THROUGH?

The rules that constitute a blocking foul at the professional levels, such as the NBA and NBA D-League, are slightly different than in college and high school, but basic concepts still apply to all levels. Whether or not the contact is marginal or incidental determines if a call will be made on the play, according to **George Toliver**, director of NBA D-League officials and former NBA official.

"We teach that a defender has to establish legal guarding position with two feet on the floor facing his opponent, and then get to the spot first in the path of the oncoming player," **Toliver** explained. "That's the guideline that makes a difference with us professionally than in college — getting into the path of the player. We are in legal guarding position if we get to the path first. If we do that prior to the offensive player getting into shooting motion, then we're in legal defense. Then it's a matter of determining on that contact if it's illegal or marginal.

"The only marginal component that comes in is the flop, which should go right to the bottom of the list in establishing whether or not we have an illegal play. If I'm in legal guarding position, I get to the spot first, and the offensive player goes to and through me, that gives the official a foundation — to and through my space — then we have a decision to make on the play. If the defensive player does his part, it's pretty easy to then adjudicate what the offensive player does. If it's a 'to and through,' then obviously we have an offensive foul. If a defensive player doesn't get into position in time, or he is sliding, or any of those things come into play, then the illegal component red flag goes up, and if there's contact, then we're dealing with a defensive foul," **Toliver** explained.

"Marginal and incidental should not be an out to just say, 'OK, there just was nothing there, it was just marginal.' We've got two bodies down and we've got a head wound, well, then that's not marginal contact. So your real cause and effect read is essentially a severity component that comes into play when that contact occurs as far as whether you're dealing with something that's illegal, marginal or incidental," **Toliver** said.

CHARGING FOUL RULES

Charging is illegal personal contact caused by pushing or moving into an opponent's torso.

• Under all codes, a player who is moving with the ball is required to stop or change direction to avoid contact if a defensive player has obtained a legal guarding position in his or her path.

• If a guard has obtained a legal guarding position, the player with the ball must get his or her head and shoulders past the torso of the defensive player. If contact occurs on the torso of the defensive player, the dribbler is responsible for the contact.

• There has to be reasonable space between two defensive players or a defensive player and the boundary line. In NFHS, if there is less than three feet of space, the dribbler has the greater responsibility for the contact. In NCAA, that space has to be sufficient to provide a reasonable chance for the dribbler to pass through without contact.

• The player with the ball may not use his or her arm or body to push the torso of the guard to gain an advantage to pass, shoot or dribble.

• A dribbler shall not charge into nor contact an opponent in his or her path nor attempt to dribble between two opponents or between an opponent and a boundary, unless the space is such as to provide a reasonable chance for him or her to go through without contact.

• If a dribbler, without contact, sufficiently passes an opponent to have head and shoulders in advance of that opponent, the greater responsibility for subsequent contact is on the opponent.

• If a dribbler in his or her progress is moving in a straight-line path, he or she may not be crowded out of that path, but if an opponent is able to legally obtain a defensive position in that path, the dribbler must avoid contact by changing direction or ending his or her dribble.

Does Turning Change the Foul?

Play: A5, team A's center, is crossing the division line while leading a three-on-two fast break. At the same time, B3 stands on the free-throw line, has both feet on the floor and has his or her torso facing A5. As the distance between A5 and B3 is getting smaller, contact between A5 and B3 is quickly becoming unavoidable. B3 recognizes the imminent contact and turns to absorb it. A5 continues to dribble and plows into turned B3. Who should the foul be on? Did B3 lose his or her legal guarding position because B3 turned? **Ruling:** B3 established legal guarding position by having his or her torso facing A5 and both feet on the floor. That guarding position didn't change even though B3 turned to absorb A5's contact. Charge A5 with a player-control foul and give team B a designated-spot throw-in on the endline. A5's foul counts toward team A's team foul count.

• The dribbler should not be permitted additional rights in executing a jump try for goal, pivoting, feinting or in starting a dribble.

• To obtain or maintain a legal rebounding position, a player may not charge an opponent or extend shoulders, hips, knees or extend the arms or elbows fully or partially in a position other than vertical so that the freedom of movement of an opponent is hindered when contact with the arms or elbows occurs.

"I think sometimes the offensive player contacts a minimal part of the defensive player (especially a player standing still) and officials end up passing on the call or penalizing the defensive player due to the minimal contact — on the defensive player's body," Barr said. "The point I'm making is the contact doesn't have to be dead center in the defensive player's chest to be a player control foul, it's the entire frame of the body when the defensive player is in his or her legal guarding position."

WHEN MOVING IS OK

We know the importance of the defense being in legal guarding position, but what does that really mean? Is the defender facing the offensive player? Does the defender have both feet on the floor when obtaining legal guarding position (unless it's NBA rules)? If so, the burden is on the player with the ball to stop or change direction in order to avoid contact.

Those are the basics, but John Lozano, instructional chair of the California Basketball Officials Association and veteran high school and women's college official, urges officials to keep other elements in mind.

"That initial guarding position doesn't require much time to be established, especially when a player has the ball," Lozano said. "Once we can understand that then the ability of a defender to maintain a legal guarding position comes into play. That means they can move to maintain a legal guarding position. They can move sideways, they can move backwards. You can't move without lifting a foot off the floor, and I demonstrate that extensively because you often hear incorrectly, 'he was moving, she was moving, the foot is off the floor.' Well, you're allowed to do that once you've established a legal guarding position and contact were to occur."

The defensive player is then allowed to stay in the path of the player with the ball and move to maintain defensive position after initially obtaining legal guarding position. In that situation, the responsibility for contact is still on the player with the ball, unless the defensive player is moving toward the player with the ball when contact occurs.

Remember too, the defender is never permitted to move into the path of an airborne offensive player. If, however, the defensive player gets to a spot first, and the offensive player then becomes airborne, the burden to avoid contact is on the offensive player. A foul in that situation would be on the offensive player.

"By now most of us have had 'referee the defense' bored into our subconscious so deeply that we by rote say, 'referee the defense,'" NBA referee **Monty McCutchen** wrote in a 6/09 *Referee* magazine article. "But what does that really mean? For years it meant for me that I should look at the defender, but that left me still being surprised at the multiple possibilities that can arise out of all the different block/charge plays. It was only after I started to watch tape more closely that I started to see patterns that I have now added to my internal dialogue as those plays start to develop. Is the defender in an equitable situation? That is, is he or she in a one-on-one defending situation in which he or she has equal talent, physical size and is in good starting position to have an advantage on those plays? If so, then my job becomes one in which I merely ask myself, 'Did he or she beat the opponent to the spot and did the offensive player go through the legally obtained space of the defender?' In short, it is not just a matter of if he or she beat them to the spot, but I must add in the sequencing of my mind that enough contact occurred to warrant a whistle. That last part is an incredibly important part of the equation. If we don't add that into our thought process, we end up with marginal contact being penalized. If both of those components occur, then I must be prepared to reward the player's hard work and bodily sacrifice."

Refereeing the defense will change your perspective and better enable you to see the whole play. By anticipating the play and focusing on the defense, you will be amazed how much easier it is to make the correct call.

BLOCK/CHARGE MECHANICS

Being in the proper position can make all the difference in getting a block/charge call right. The responsibilities for officials vary in two-person and three-person mechanics, so it's important to know where you need to be on the court to make the right call when the situation develops.

THREE-PERSON CONCEPTS

With three officials on the court, the chances of being in position to make a block/charge call are far greater than with two officials because movements by the officials don't leave open gaps in coverage.

It is important to remember that all three officials must work hard at understanding and obtaining proper angles in calling a block/charge. You must be able to see completely through the play, which means your vision must be unobstructed by the players directly involved in the play and others near the play.

Basketball is a game of nearly constant motion. An official's angle and distance adjustments are necessary as play is in motion. A step or two in the right direction may open up a whole new viewing experience, free from obstruction; a step in the wrong direction will screen you from the critical game action.

Movement is needed in three-person officiating, just like in two-person crews. Unlike in two-person officiating, moving far onto the court is generally a three-person no-no. With only two officials, the trail must constantly be on the court to cover plays on the other side of the court. Not so with three officials. Almost all of the trail and center's movement will be away or toward the endlines, not toward the center of the court.

The lead also moves along the endline to improve angles. There's usually at least four and sometimes six or eight players in the lane area battling for position. Lead movement is critical to watching low-post action, but it can be paramount to seeing a secondary defender in a block/charge situation.

"If you are out of position, straightlined, you're not going to be able to see this," said **Lozano**. "The less information you have, the less you have to go with to make a quick decision. Very likely you're making the wrong decision because you don't have enough information to make a decision based on your knowledge. We try to demonstrate if you're the lead official if you're straightlined you're not going to see that block/charge. If you're not refereeing the defense, same kind of thing.

"We have to make adjustments to release the responsibility if you're the outer official, the trail official, to the lead official," said **Lozano**. "You have to release a little bit sooner, especially if the lead official is in position. I think communication and where you pick up the ball, you have to work with a little bit more and establish those guidelines, where you're going to do that and who's going to pick up the ball."

In nearly all cases, the lead official triggers movements (rotations) by the other two officials. Well-timed, distinct movements by the lead make for smooth rotations and great court coverage.

Toliver says that determining each component of a play that is developing from start to finish will help you react in time to make the right call.

"If you're looking at the offensive player, then you're not going to know if the defensive player is in legal guarding position," **Toliver** said. "That's the key player in judging this scenario here. Referee the defensive player first to determine if he or she has done the things that makes him or her legal. It's really pretty cut and dried; it's something that's trainable. You throw in a component of having a patient whistle, letting the play process, let it start, develop, finish, and now you're just really refereeing that moment of impact. But you're refereeing that moment of impact with a knowledge that defensive player either was or was not in legal guarding position when that contact occurred."

TWO-PERSON CONCEPTS

Both officials must work a little harder at obtaining proper angles to make a block/charge call. Your line of sight must provide you with an opportunity to view a developing play or part of a play. You must be able to see completely through the play, which means your vision must be unobstructed by the players directly involved in the play and others near the play.

With two officials, the trail must move off (away from) the sideline for proper court coverage. Far too often officials who can't (or won't) run well stay on the sideline near halfcourt. They're afraid of getting in the way and aren't confident they can move quickly enough to avoid passing lanes and get good angles. The game suffers because court coverage suffers. A good trail official moves off the near sideline when the ball is nearer the far sideline, sometimes to the middle of the court between the free throw circle and center circle, to get good angles and proper distance from the play.

Why such an emphasis on trail movement? That allows the lead to watch players off-ball, the critical component to combating physical play. When the trail moves off the sideline to cover plays, the lead can focus on the lane area and be in position for a block/charge call.

BASIC FRONTCOURT COVERAGE
THREE PERSON

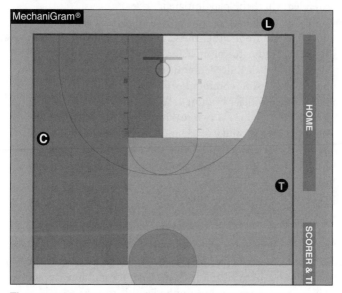

Three-person crews must understand their positions and obtain proper angles for calling a block/charge.

When the ball is in the frontcourt, each official is responsible for observing an area of the floor. Those areas of coverage don't change regardless if you're on the ball or off ball, and a block/charge could happen in any of those areas.

In a halfcourt setting, the trail's responsibilities include the area to the far free-throw lane line extended, above the free-throw line, to the division line and the sideline nearest the trail.

The center's responsibilities include the area from the near free-throw lane line extended to the division line, the sideline nearest the center and half of the lane itself.

The lead's responsibilities include half of the lane, free-throw line extended to the three-point arc, down to the endline on the lead's side of the court.

During frontcourt action in three-person mechanics, the center official often is responsible for dribble drives to the goal that initiate that coverage area. That's where a block/charge often will occur. Pregaming this situation is a must. Some feel it is best for the center who has a drive from start to finish to make the call on a block/charge. Others feel the lead should take it, even if he or she is opposite the free throw line extended where the play initiated.

"I absolutely harp on our officials not to be calling block/charges from either the C or the T," said **Art Hyland**, Big East coordinator of men's basketball officials and NCAA Men's Basketball Rules Committee secretary-rules editor. "I'm talking about stuff coming down the lane now. I really believe that the lead official in those cases has the best chance of getting them right, for two reasons, especially when you're dealing with a secondary defender. If you are the trail or you are the center official and a play starts in front of you and the dribbler beats his man, you should be refereeing those two players — that dribbler and that primary defender. There is no way you should be watching in the lane for a help defender or secondary defender. Now all of a sudden you have this play and it gets to the lane line, and there's a help defender there and you're now going to try to make a determination whether he was there or whether he was still moving. Meanwhile the lead who has been sitting back there on the end line can see this help defender coming and he has a better chance of getting it right than the officials from out front. We try to get the lead official on most plays inside the foul line coming down the lane to leave it for the lead to take."

Others believe that the center has watched that play from the start, understanding who had better position, whether or not the defender obtained legal guarding position, watched the initiation of the drive to see if the dribbler did anything illegal, etc. If the lead is doing his or her job properly, there's no way he or she could referee the defense and make a sound judgment, especially when the drive starts from the center's free-throw line extended area.

"It depends on where the play originated from and if there is a secondary defender," says **Struckhoff**. "It could originate in the C's area and if the C has the primary defender the whole way, then I think the C has the best chance of getting that right. If it initiates on the C's side and it goes to the basket and now we've got a secondary defender sliding over, I think the lead has the best chance of getting that right."

In certain cases, the center must be aggressive in making a block/charge call. It's perfectly fine for the center to sell a blocking foul or bang out a player-control foul that occurs near the low block. He or she may have had the best look from start to finish.

BLOCK/CHARGE

If you find yourself in the center position and ready to make that call, get a great angle on the play, referee the defense and penetrate at least a step toward the play as you make your signal.

Depending on where the foul occurred, the lead may be closer to the collision, but did not have the best look at it because of the players in between, so in that case, it's the center's play all the way.

TWO PERSON

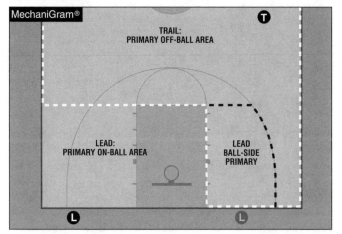

MechaniGram®

T

TRAIL:
PRIMARY OFF-BALL AREA

LEAD:
PRIMARY ON-BALL AREA

LEAD
BALL-SIDE
PRIMARY

L   **L**

The ability to see completely through a play with unobstructed vision is essential to pick up players directly involved and others near the play.

In the frontcourt, basic coverage shifts depending on which official is on-ball.

The lead's on-ball responsibilities include the area below the free-throw line extended to the far edge of the free-throw lane line (away from the lead) when the lead is opposite the trail and the floor is balanced. If the lead is ball-side, the lead's area of responsibility grows. It includes the area below the free-throw line extended to the the three-point arc.

When the lead is on-ball, the trail's off-ball responsibilities include the area above the free-throw line extended to the division line and the lane area from the free-throw lane line (nearest the trail) to the sideline nearest the trail. The trail's off-ball area of responsibility decreases when the lead is on-ball, ball-side. It is the area above the free-throw line extended and outside the three-point arc.

Officials are responsible for a five-second count within their primary coverage area. If the ball moves out of the official's primary area, that official should remain with that count until it is ended. Once the count has ended, return to your primary coverage area.

DRIVES, FAST-BREAK RESPONSIBILITIES

THREE PERSON

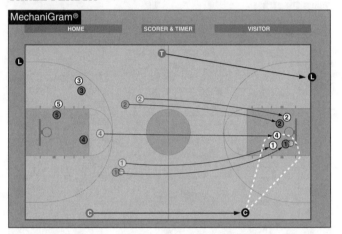

Fast-break action is shared among the lead and center officials, and they are responsible for action that originates from their side of the lane.

Fast-break action is shared among the new lead and center officials. Trainers will often drill the phrase into the heads of referees: "Don't get beat back." In three-person officiating, the new lead or previous trail usually has a much better opportunity to beat the play to the other end after a quick steal or turnover and make a ruling on a block/charge.

Much like frontcourt drives to the basket, the lead and center officials are responsible for action that originates from their side of the lane, even on fast breaks. However, as the MechaniGram on the opposite page illustrates, the new lead is blocked by other players and can't get a proper look to see the drive to the basket. The center official must officiate the action and call any foul that has been committed, including a block/charge call beneath the low block.

Move in to get the proper angles depending upon how far away from the play you may be. If a crash is imminent, stop your movement and get a good look at the play. If a block/charge has occurred, hustle in closer and make the signal as necessary.

TWO PERSON

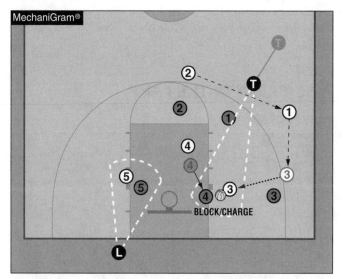

MechaniGram®

BLOCK/CHARGE

Good trail movement in a two-person crew allows the lead to watch players off-ball and to be in position for a potential block/charge.

Sometimes, the lead doesn't have enough time to get ballside and get a good look on drives toward the basket. When players make quick passes away from the lead that cover a great distance, it's difficult to react in time to get a good angle.

When that happens, there's a simple solution: "You take the stuff on your side of the hoop and I'll take the stuff on my side of the hoop."

When the lead is on the far side of the court, the trail has a much better look on drives to the lane that start on the trail's half of the court. But it takes an aggressive, hard-working trail to make the call correctly and with conviction, even though the play is going toward the lead.

In the MechaniGram (on previous page), the officials start the play with the floor balanced. Team A throws a quick swing pass and that player quickly drives to the basket. The action is too fast for the lead to move ball side. As the drive to the basket occurs, the secondary defender steps in to take a charge. The trail penetrates toward the endline, gets a good angle and makes the judgment on the contact.

Developing an aggressive mind-set as a trail official will help overall court coverage. Don't leave the lead alone. Do your part by taking the action on your side of the basket when the lead can't see clearly.

PASS/CRASH IN THE LANE

THREE PERSON

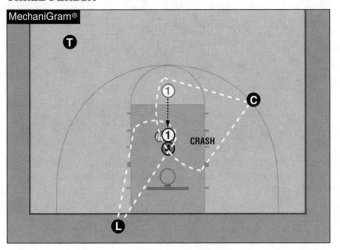

Pregaming responsibilities on any drive to the basket is a must with a three-person crew.

A player driving a crowded lane, passing off to a teammate, then crashing into a defender can be one of the most difficult plays to officiate because there is so much going on in a small area in a short period of time.

In a three-person crew it becomes a bit easier because of the additional set of eyes. If the passer sends the ball out toward the trail, the trail will follow the ball and the center and lead will stay with the crash. If the ball is passed out toward the center's side of the floor, the center will follow the ball while the trail and lead momentarily stay with the crash.

If you are the center or the trail official, penetrate down toward the endline to get a better view of the play, but be aware of the kickout pass and make sure you're not too close to an ensuing three-point attempt.

And as the lead official, once you determine that a drive down the lane is imminent, move toward the close-down position along the lane line (as shown in the MechaniGram on the opposite page) to get a better view of the activity in the lane.

TWO PERSON

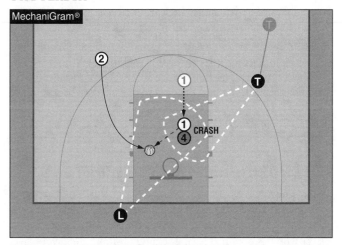

By penetrating toward the endline when a player drives the lane, the trail can take some of the pressure off the lead by being in great position to judge the play.

For the lead, a player driving a crowded lane, passing off to a teammate, then crashing into a defender is tough to handle alone. Did the passer get fouled? Did the passer foul? Block? Charge? Is it a team or player-control foul? Did the dribbler travel? Did the player filling the lane catch the pass cleanly and travel or did the player merely fumble and recover? Did the violation occur before the foul? That's way too much for one official to handle in most cases.

The trail must help. By aggressively penetrating toward the endline when players drive the lane, the trail can take some of the pressure off the lead by being in great position to judge the play.

The common phrase that sums up responsibilities is, "Lead takes the pass, trail takes the crash." That's generally accurate when the pass is toward the lead. However, when the pass is toward the trail (especially out toward the perimeter), the trail should take the pass and the lead take the crash.

The trail should watch the dribbler penetrate. Watch for the dribbler being fouled on the drive or while passing. Also, the trail watches for the dribbler crashing into a defender after releasing a pass that goes toward the lead. Referee the defense to see if the defender obtained legal guarding position. Be especially wary of dribblers who leave their feet to make a pass. Don't bail out an out-of-control player with a no-call.

With the trail watching that action, the lead can concentrate primarily on the pass toward the lead and the player receiving it. Don't fall into the trap, however, of leaving all crashes to the trail. For the lead, the pass is primary, but the crash is secondary. You'd rather have a call on the crash from the lead than a no-call that lets a foul get away. Make a call as the lead if you have to.

DEFENDER/PIVOT PLAYER RIGHTS

When a pivot player is being guarded, he or she should expect to be guarded as closely as possible from all sides. When he or she turns or rises to shoot and makes contact with a defensive player who has obtained legal guarding position, the pivot player has committed a foul. Do not penalize the defensive player if the player did nothing illegal. The defensive player is entitled to jump vertically from a legally obtained position on the court and is entitled to occupy the space within the vertical plane. The defensive player did nothing improper by leaving the floor from a legally established guarding position.

Merely jumping straight up in the air to block a shot is not illegal. Look to see which player caused the contact. If the offensive player's body or hands cause the contact with a defensive player who jumps in the air, which frequently happens since players are coached to "go strong to the basket," then it is a no call or a foul on the offensive player if the contact is such that an advantage is gained by the offense, or the defensive player is placed at a disadvantage. The offensive player may not break the plane of the defensive player. Look to see which player causes the contact and the call is easy.

THE HOLLYWOOD FLOP

PlayPic®

A flop should jump out at you when determining who initiated contact.

By rule, pretending to be charged into (the flop) is unsporting conduct and subject to a technical foul. About 22 years ago, a high school game in Louisiana featured six such technical fouls called. Today, it's not very prominent and undoubtedly you won't see it called very often. However, the flopper's presence on the floor can present a danger to other players, and blatant flopping, particularly when there is zero contact, needs to be addressed. If a warning to the coach will not fix the situation, call the technical foul.

Floppers have become good. Very good. Coaches teach, players practice and it has become a necessary evil in the game. But instead of handing out Academy Awards, address the situation. Put a stop to it early.

What about the case in which there is some contact and the defender overreacts by staggering backward or even falling, trying to make a case for a foul call (see PlayPic)?

If the flopper puts him or herself at a disadvantage before the official has a legitimate chance to determine whether contact initiated by an opponent would have resulted in any disadvantage, there can be no foul called. (Remember we are not talking about an obvious crash.) Err on the side of legitimate play.

"Flopping should be down at the bottom in your thinking, not at the top," said **Toliver**. "When you referee the defense and you see a player's position and if that player sits down, flops, that should stand out to you, it really shouldn't be a part of your top-level thinking. Top-level thinking should be: Is the defensive player legal or illegal?

"Let the flop jump out at you. Don't think, well, this is a flopper, so they're going to flop, or there's a tendency to flop. It's very risky to put that at the top. If you referee the defense and you make determinations of whether they're legal or

BLOCK/CHARGE

illegal, that would be a case where that's going to jump out at you. If you handle that defensive player the right way, a lot of things just fall right into place, flopping included," **Toliver** said.

Other hints of theatrical activity can be observed, like loud shouts or grunts to get sympathy. The direction of the flop can sometimes be a clue. Any reaction that is not in line with the direction of the contact is suspect.

BLOCK/CHARGE CHECKLIST

✓ Blocking is illegal personal contact which impedes the progress of an opponent with or without the ball and shall be penalized.

✓ Charging is illegal personal contact caused by pushing or moving into an opponent's torso.

✓ A player can legally hold his or her hands and arms in front of his or her face or body for protection and to absorb force from an imminent charge by an opponent in an attempt to draw a player control foul.

✓ In the NBA, players are required to get their torso into position. Moving their feet sideways or backwards is OK, like in NFHS and NCAA, after obtaining legal guarding position.

✓ A player shall not push, hold, trip or impede the progress of an opponent by extending his or her arm(s), hip(s) or knee(s) or by bending his or her own body into other than a normal position while guarding an opponent.

✓ A secondary defender is a teammate who has helped a primary defender after that player has been beaten by an opponent because he failed to establish or maintain a legal guarding position.

✓ Know where you need to be on the court in three-person and two-person mechanics to make the right call when the situation develops.

✓ Referee the defense. Is the defender facing the offensive player? Does the defender have both feet on the floor (unless it's NBA rules)?

✓ Know the verticality rules and rights of the defender and pivot player.

✓ A flopper's presence on the floor can present a danger to other players. Blatant flopping, particularly when there is zero contact, needs to be addressed.

CH3

CHAPTER 3

CONTACT/ DISPLACEMENT

Guidelines have been established at all levels to help coaches, players and officials achieve a level of play that will allow freedom of movement for all players on the court. When that freedom of movement is disrupted with handchecking, rough post play or illegal screens, it's up to the officials to enforce those guidelines to ensure that freedom of movement is permitted in the game.

Officials at all levels have improved over the years at calling displacement, especially in the post area, but it is still a point of emphasis for some codes.

"I think our game is not nearly the low post wrestling match that it was three, four, five years ago," says **John Adams**, NCAA national coordinator for men's basketball officials. "I think officials have tuned into that by adjudicating and officiating plays involving dislodgement very quickly and consistently. Since no coach wants his big man out of the game, when he picks up his first foul, everybody's paying attention.

"I think enforcing three seconds has helped also," **Adams** says. "If we don't let them stand in there, it's hard to stand in there and wrestle."

In this chapter we'll examine various forms of contact, including opinions from leaders in the basketball officiating community on contact on the perimeter and post, verticality and other types of contact.

THE RULES

CONTACT

In all codes, a player shall not hold, push, charge, trip; nor impede the progress of an opponent by extending an arm, shoulder, hip or knee, or by bending the body into other than a normal position; nor use any rough tactics.

• A player shall not contact an opponent with his/her hand unless such contact is only with the opponent's hand while it is on the ball and is incidental to an attempt to play the ball .

• A player shall not use his/her hands on an opponent in any way that inhibits the freedom of movement of the opponent or acts as an aid to a player in starting or stopping. That includes the offensive post player from holding, hooking or displacing the leg or body of the defender. It also is illegal contact for a post player to "back down" and displace the defender once that defender has established a legal guarding position.

• A player shall not extend the arm(s) fully or partially other than vertically so that freedom of movement of an opponent is hindered when contact or displacement occurs from a locked and/or extended elbow.

• A player shall not use an arm-bar and/or hand to prevent an opponent from attacking the ball during a dribble or when throwing for goal. It also is illegal contact for a player to use the "swim stroke" arm movement to lower the arm of an opponent.

• Contact caused by a defensive player who approaches from behind is pushing. It is illegal contact when an airborne rebounder is undercut and displaced. Contact caused by the momentum of a player who has thrown for a goal is a form of charging.

• A player shall adhere to the rules pertaining to illegal contact as related to guarding, rebounding, screening and verticality.

"We owe it to the rebounder to protect him," **Adams** said. "Summer basketball is very, very ripe with players trying to strip the rebounders without calls. When you get into college, you're used to do that — swatting, slapping, grabbing a rebounder as he has the ball. By instinct he turns hard to get away from that pressure or swings his elbows to get away from that pressure. Now if he hits a legal defender and he is just standing there, that's a whole different issue than a defender who is slapping, grabbing and pulling the guy's arm trying to dislodge the rebound."

NCAA WOMEN EXCEPTION

While most contact rules are similar between high school, college and the professional levels, there is a difference between NCAA men and women when it comes to displacement, especially with handchecks.

A post player in NCAA women's basketball is defined as any offensive or defensive player in the lane area with or without the ball with her back to the basket. The lane area includes the three-second lane and approximately three feet just outside the lane. An offensive post player becomes a ballhandler when, while in the lane area, she turns and faces the basket with the ball or moves completely outside the lane area with the ball.

"If my back is to the basket, you can have an arm in my back and the normal rules apply," said **Debbie Williamson**, secretary-rules editor for NCAA women's basketball. "As long as you don't displace me, pull, push me, not allow me freedom of movement, hold, that sort of thing. If you do any of those things it's still illegal, but now once I grab the ball and face the basket we have a more stringent set of rules, and that is keep your hands off the dribbler. Then the determination becomes did the dribbler create the contact or did the defense, which is the case for 94 feet."

NCAA women are allowed to "measure up" a ballhandler or dribbler once. It is also known as the "hot stove" touch. Any hand contact beyond that is a foul. If the defender contacts the ballhandler/dribbler at anytime with two hands, an arm-bar or "body bumps," it is illegal contact and a foul.

"Does it have a bearing on the play; did it prevent someone from scoring a basket; did it prevent someone from making a cut to run their offensive move; did it disrupt speed, balance, quickness and rhythm; did it displace; did it hold; did it take somebody out of their principal verticality; did it take somebody out of their straight line pass toward the bucket, whether you've got the ball or don't have the ball," said **Patty Broderick**, coordinator of the Women's Basketball Officiating Consortium, which includes seven Division I conferences and one Division II conference, and a former NCAA and WNBA official. "You've got to put all those things into the equation to decide whether you have a no call or you have a foul. In the women's game we have a few fouls that are automatic, which you don't need displacement. You cannot handcheck. You cannot use an arm-bar. Those are touch fouls. You get one hot stove touch and then if you poke back again and again, hands on all the time or multiple touches, those are fouls and that doesn't take displacement. Those are kind of like tagging fouls. Then the arm-bar, you can't touch them with an extended arm-bar at all on the ballhandler/dribbler.

"Those are absolute fouls," **Broderick** said. "In the women's game we have absolutes on handchecking and extended arm-bar on the ballhandler/dribbler."

INCIDENTAL CONTACT

Incidental contact is contact with an opponent which is permitted and which does not constitute a foul. The mere fact that contact occurs does not mean a player has committed a foul. When 10 players are moving rapidly in a limited area, some contact is certain to occur.

Contact that is incidental to an effort by an opponent to reach a loose ball, or contact which may result when opponents are in equally favorable positions to perform normal defensive or offensive movements, should not be considered illegal, even though the contact may be severe or excessive.

"Body contact is often incidental," said **John Lozano**, instructional chair of the California Basketball Officials Association and veteran high school and women's college official. "You're going to have two players making contact with each other. I start to draw the line when the arms reach out and start putting their hand on the defender. There's almost a foot of space, two feet of space, but the arm is out there. I look for a lot of arm extension because those arms do seem to impact the offensive player. I look for displacement. I think when I'm inside the key you're going to have a lot more solid, strong body contact. But if displacement is occurring and I think the arm and upper body motion seem to be engaged ... I'm not one to preach the light tap foul, especially because there's plenty of harder fouls, more obvious fouls that occur. I guess probably on the perimeter I see more arm activity to observe, and as you get close into the paint the motions with the body and what appears to be some sort of displacement."

Contact which does not hinder the opponent from participating in normal defensive or offensive movements should be considered incidental.

A player who is screened within his/her visual field is expected to avoid contact with the screener by stopping or going around the screener. In cases of screens outside the visual field, the opponent may make inadvertent contact with the screener, and such contact is to be ruled incidental contact, provided the screener is not displaced if he/she has the ball.

If, however, a player approaches an opponent from behind or from a position from which he/she has no reasonable chance to play the ball without making contact with the opponent, the responsibility is on the player in the unfavorable position.

Every player is entitled to a spot on the playing court, provided the player gets there first without illegally contacting an opponent.

"The incidental contact rule is probably one of the oldest rules in the game of basketball," said **Art Hyland**, NCAA Men's Basketball Rules Committee secretary-rules editor and Big East coordinator of men's basketball officials. "It basically allows some kind of contact to be legal as long as it does not disadvantage one side or the other. And it could be serious contact. If you have two 6-foot-5, 250-pound players with equal access to a rebound and they crash into each other and they hit the floor, that's not a foul. I'm not talking about somebody going from behind and shoving a guy, I'm talking about from the side and they're both going to the ball. That's not a foul, according to the incidental contact rule.

ROUGH PLAY

"There are a few things that are now absolutes," **Hyland** said. "In my mind, an absolute is every time a certain thing occurs, you call it. I think we have to be careful. The two rules seem to be in opposition in some ways to each other. There are certain things which the rules committee over the past 10 years has been trying to get out of the game and they all involve rough play. They involve handchecking, and with regard to handchecking we have said that there are certain guidelines and when those occur you're supposed to call them all the time, not just once or twice early in the game. The same thing with body bumping. When I start to turn the corner on you and you keep your hands back and they're not on me, but you come up and bump me with your stomach and your chest as I try to turn the corner, it's another type of handcheck. Those are disadvantageous and the rules committee has tried to get that out of the game for about 10 years, ever since a point of emphasis has been to eliminate physical play. That's been one of the things we're trying to get rid of also. A third thing is the illegal screen. Quite honestly I think we're starting to call more illegal screens, but there's a lot more that occur during the game than we're all calling. There has to be a renewed significant effort to try to get more of those calls. If you watch the average college game, at least in Division I, most everybody is using the pick and roll. That's an integral part of their offense. You're going to see 30 to 50 screens a game. It's going to be coming at you, one after the other, sometimes two or three within 10 seconds, screens all over the place."

To be consistent each official and his or her crew members need to adopt the following three disciplines:

• Be in position to observe both the severity of the contact and who initiated it.

• Withhold any whistle until the play is completed.

• Observe the result of the contact in its entirety and then, and only then, make a final judgment on the play. That may require the official to change his or her first impression, which may be the most difficult thing to do in the very short time period available.

A slow whistle is critical. So is a feel for the game to determine whether the player contacted ("bumpee") was placed at a disadvantage or the "bumper" gained an advantage. Further, those disciplines apply at all levels of play, for both genders and for differences in the size of the players.

VERTICALITY

Verticality applies to a legal position. The basic components of the principle of verticality are:

• A legal guarding position must be attained initially and movement thereafter must be legal.

• From that position, the defender may rise or jump vertically and occupy the space within his or her vertical plane.

Post players are usually going to compete for floor position prior to a rebound, and the official must be vigilant and see who violates the principle of verticality, especially when it comes to rebounding. That means diverting attention from the ball toward the floor and body positions of the rebounding players.

• The hands and arms of the defender may be raised within his or her vertical plane while on the floor or in the air.

• The defender should not be penalized for leaving the floor vertically or having his or her hands and arms extended within his or her vertical plane.

"I think that can get confusing, as we've been taught with the block/charge, to referee the defense," says **Mary Struckhoff**, an NFHS assistant director, basketball rules interpreter, editor and NCAA national coordinator of women's basketball officiating. "If we continue to referee the defense and we have a good look at the defense, we may miss the offensive player violating the principle of verticality if we don't get a good look at it."

Simply put, the defender is not locked to the ground. The opportunity is there to move up and down (vertically) without being pushed or forced out of the way. Any contact judged severe enough to warrant a foul should not be called on the defender in such a situation. It is tough to understand and even tougher to judge, but the defender can jump and be airborne while still maintaining a legally vertical position.

If the contact was severe enough to warrant a foul call, you're in perfect position to call the player-control foul if the defender indeed held his ground. If the contact was minimal and had little effect on the play, no-call the play and move on. But there are other movements by the defender to look for on the play, according to Hyland.

"I personally feel that the verticality rule has made our game somewhat uglier than it should be," **Hyland** said. "The only thing I can go back to is when I played in college, which was a long time ago. Even when I coached in the late '60s and early '70s, if a player went up for a shot and he got his arm hit, that was a foul. You went to the line for two shots. Then we got the verticality rule. The verticality rule basically says that if I as a defender have established legal guarding position and I have my hands pretty much straight up in the air and the guy goes to take a jump shot and his elbow goes into my arm, it's not a foul. If I have my arms pretty much straight up in the air and I've established legal guarding position before that, I've done nothing wrong, so it's not a foul.

"Players are now taught to get their arms straight up in the air," **Hyland** said. "A lot of times as the player is shooting, the defender is putting his hands from around his waist area to straight up in the air. He hits the guy on the way up, but when the play ends his hands are above his head. Those are fouls, but they're hard to see because at the end of the play you see the defender with his hands straight up over his head. A lot of times the defender really doesn't get his hands straight up there, they're a little bit at an angle. There's nothing definitive. So sometimes they're at an angle and sometimes it's pretty far down, almost perpendicular to your body, those are clearly fouls. But how straight do they have to be before it's a legal play? Those are all judgments that officials have to make and you end up with a lot

PlayPic®

From an initial guarding position, the defender may rise or jump vertically and occupy the space within his/her vertical plane.

of ugly plays. If a guy goes up for a shot and goes into the defender's arms, and the ball goes flying someplace and the official passes on it because he thinks it's a legal verticality play. So they're very hard plays.

"The only thing that I try to emphasize is this idea of getting your hands up in the air," **Hyland** said. "I'd like to have them pretty straight. The more you allow them to come at an angle, the more that becomes an illegal play."

• The offensive player whether on the floor or airborne, may not "clear out" or cause contact within the defender's vertical plane which is a foul. When officiating post play, where most blocked shots occur, focus on the defender before the ball is fed inside. That allows you to determine whether or not initial legal guarding position has been obtained. Refereeing the defense provides the foundation for making the correct call on the ensuing blocked shot attempt. Next, anticipate that the defender will make a clean block rather than anticipating contact. That mind-set requires a patient whistle. By anticipating no whistle, you've given yourself time to see the entire play and then make your decision.

• The defender may not "belly up" or use the lower part of the body or arms to cause contact outside his or her vertical plane which is a foul.

Defensive players have become well-schooled in moving the offensive player out of the post while remaining vertical from the waist up. By using a hip, knee or stomach, the defender is able to "belly up" the offensive player. Most often, that will force the offensive player farther from the basket, while creating a decided advantage for the defensive player. That foul must be called.

• The player with the ball is to be given no more protection or consideration than the defender in judging which player has violated the rules.

PERIMETER CONTACT

HANDCHECKING

Handchecks have often been mentioned among the specific points of emphasis in reference to rough play while "body bumping" has served as an alternative to handchecking for some defenders. Both types of fouls are typically not very rough, but can make all the difference between an offensive player getting a shot off or making a drive to the basket.

Many officials struggle with when a handcheck is truly a foul versus when it's a passing tap that can be ignored. Officials can let the game down by choosing to draw the line between foul and no foul in the wrong place. We base our decision on our own degree of comfort with the reaction we inevitably draw from the participants. We shouldn't let their misunderstanding of the intent of the rule keep us from calling that foul consistently. And to call it consistently, we have to look at tactical advantage and intent.

Officials should call a handcheck when it's used by the defense as an effective substitute for strong body position or when it's used to goad the opponent. Quite often, however, officials look the other way when a handcheck occurs.

"It's terrible. The better the players, the more there is," says **Lozano**. "Maybe I should say it differently, but the teams that seem to be very successful at the high school level play with more contact. That's OK, it is a contact sport. I noticed that early in the year because those guys practice between themselves during the offseason and during the early practices in the fall before the season starts, so they're accustomed to not having people call things. Their coaches might be their referees during scrimmages and intra-squads, but they probably don't do a great job and the players don't listen to them anyway. When we're finally starting to either officiate their scrimmages as officials or do their practice games, or we have opportunities where we have our own practice sessions for officials and we're able to utilize a couple of teams to do that, what I notice is that everybody is very fuzzy and rusty on contact. The better teams do a lot more contact, more handchecking. The better officials are better at calling it, but the average official almost doesn't see it, and I don't understand that. It's an area that we address and we talk about."

A defender can commit a handcheck foul off-ball just as easily as he or she can while guarding a ballhandler/dribbler. One way is when the defender is guarding an opponent who is weak side to the ball. In other words, if the ball is on the left wing and the offensive player is on the right side of the paint and being guarded by a defender in the lane, a handcheck by that defender can be used as an effective — and illegal — tool to keep track of the offensive player. It eliminates some of the element of surprise by a sudden back-door cut to the hoop. Above all else, it's a lot easier to play defense by feel than having to keep an eye on the person being guarded.

But most handchecking fouls occur when the defender is attempting to disrupt the ballhandler/dribbler, especially a guard who often attempts to penetrate the lane area.

"There are two plays," said **Curtis Shaw**, former NCAA basketball official who is coordinator of officials for Conference USA, Big 12, Southland and Ohio Valley conferences and is also coordinator of women's basketball officials for the Ohio Valley and Atlantic Sun conferences. "I allow a player to touch with a hand to measure up. Once they've measured up, any continuous touching with the hand, or any touching with the hand which guides the dribbler or impedes the dribbler from turning, we have to have a foul. If a guy is making a move east and west and he's just going cross-court and there's some slight touching, measuring up with the hand, we're OK. But the minute the player tries to make a move toward the basket and there's a hand or a forearm still on him, you've got to have the defensive foul. Even if he's able to go ahead and beat him, because if not he might push him wider than he wanted to go, any number of things could've occurred. But if we were just making it automatic, if a man is going north and south and he gets touched with a hand for more than the first time of just measuring up, we need a foul."

Another obvious use of a handcheck by a defender is to negate the effect of an effective screen by the offense. If a player sees a screen coming and can extend his or her reach past the screen, it can produce some delaying effect on an attacker's movement to an open spot on the floor. In such a case, you've got a handcheck as well.

Notice that the way we've described a handcheck here avoids reference to holding, blocking and various infringements on verticality by the defense. The handcheck is basically a "transition" foul that the defender uses to an illegal advantage to keep from being put in a position of committing those other fouls. It is often misconstrued as a synonym for those other fouls. When you understand it in that context, it gets a lot easier to understand when a handcheck is justified to call and when it isn't.

For instance, if a dribbler is above the arc and moving across the court, a temporary touch by the defender, who is turning to guard the dribbler, may have no practical effect on the play because the defender doesn't need body position in such a case. That might be a good time to pass on calling a foul, but it leads us to the second case of when to call hand checks - the nuisance foul.

There no doubt are coaches who teach their players to lay a hand on the backside of the player they're guarding at every opportunity they can get away with. They do it simply to create an annoyance, a distraction or worse as a way of creating an advantage and they will go on doing it until somebody stops them. Put a stop to all that before the players start taking matters into their own hands, because a small match can often ignite a mighty forest fire. Deal with chronic handchecks whether they're an extension of guarding position or not.

"We just have to constantly monitor it and remind our officials that we can't get complacent," **Lozano** said. "It is good that teams are able to adjust when we make calls. I see that, and the better teams definitely will make the adjustment. If it's a rough, physical game, they have to play rough and physical. If we try to tighten up the game a little bit, the better teams seem to make adjustments and you just really hope that you don't make an adjustment as an official by the third quarter instead of earlier on once it's clear that we have to focus on more of the contact that's occurring."

The official has two basic ways of taking action on handchecks. If they pop up as individual incidents, such as a prevention of a move to the basket, then treat them like any other foul and call them. On the other hand, you can often eliminate the weak-side checks and nuisance fouls with a voice that can be heard in the immediate area of the players involved, like "Straight up!" or "Hands!" The smart players will heed a warning and clean up their defense before it starts contributing to the foul count. If they decide not to listen or just can't help themselves, then jump on it early in the game. It's amazing how one "message" call early on can clear the situation up for the rest of the evening.

"Some crews in women's college basketball continue to permit continuous and illegal contact by the defender on the ballhandler/dribbler as she drives to the basket," said **Struckhoff**. "It is imperative that officials make that call early in the game so that players and coaches understand how the game is going to be called and can make the proper adjustments. Any impede, displacement or re-route of that dribbler is a foul and must be called."

BODY BUMPING

As officials try to put a lid on handchecks, defenders have turned to use their torso as a way to guide a ballhandler/dribbler instead of their hands, especially on the perimeter. Defenders will run alongside a ballhandler/dribbler with their hands straight up in the air, but at the same time make contact with the ballhandler/dribbler with their hips.

"What they are doing is body bumping," said **Dave Libbey**, West Coast Conference coordinator of men's basketball officials and a former NCAA official. "If I put my hands in the air and bump you one or two times and push you out, the defender can still stay in front of the ballhandler. They think they're getting away with something and we're starting to pick it up.

"The perimeter is a crucial part of the game," **Libbey** said. "If you've got a guard kind of turned and they're trying to penetrate so they can get help weak-side and dish off, that's a good play. But if the defender is bumping the ballhandler out and he can't penetrate, the defense is messing with the offense's whole scheme to get the play off."

SCREENS

Screening principles consistently challenge officials season after season. They continually occur throughout the game and, unless you see the entire play, your chances of getting it right are a guess at best. So in an effort to give you a better than 50-50 chance, let's explore all the intricacies of a legal screen.

A blind or back screen that is not set properly is a blocking foul when illegal contact occurs.

By definition, screens are legal actions if set properly. If not, it's usually a blocking foul when illegal contact occurs. Sound simple? Judge for yourself after you review the following guidelines:

The intent of a screen is to delay or prevent an opponent from reaching a given spot on the court and must be accomplished without causing contact. Although most screens are set by the offense, they may be employed by the defense.

A player with the ball may also be a screener and is subject to the same guidelines. In order to establish a legal screening position:

• The screener may face any direction.

• Time and distance may be factors.

• The screener must be stationary (unless both opponents are moving in the same path and direction).

There are certain differences that come into play when screening a stationary opponent, as opposed to screening a moving opponent. First, the following applies to screening a stationary opponent:

• When a screen is set from the front or side, the screener may be as close as possible, short of contact.

• When a screen is set from the rear, the opponent must be allowed one normal step backward without contact.

Those two aspects are the most important parts of the definition for officials to know regarding the ball screen at the top of the key. Officials have to know where the screen is set on the defender to properly adjudicate the play. Without it, you're guessing.

Hedging by the defender is designed to impede the progress of the offense. It's a tactic being taught by coaches that is again becoming popular at all levels of basketball.

For a defender to "jump" the screen legally, he or she must anticipate the movement of the offensive player and obtain a legal guarding position. If that initial guarding position is obtained, then any contact that occurs would be the responsibility of the offensive player.

Defensive players that jump out on the screen to body bump or hedge the offensive player must be called for a foul. Even a slight bump can affect the offensive player's balance or the speed of the play. If freedom of movement was compromised, a foul must be called.

Who will see that play? In a two-person crew, the lead might need to extend his or her coverage area to help officiate that play. If the trail has an extensive amount of ball pressure, it will be difficult for him or her to turn away. In a three-person crew, the center official will have a great look at the initial set-up of the screener and the ensuing contact.

"What we've seen more is the hedge play where the big guy comes out and hedges up on the little guard and throws a leg out there," said **Libbey**. "If there's contact, that's a foul.

"As far as the screen, the player has to be stationary. If he or she is not or pushes a knee out, it's a foul," Libbey said. "If the defense is guarding the offense and able to stay with him or her and he or she goes up for a shot and the defender is right there, he or she has a chance to block it. If that defender is picked and knocked off his area of speed, balance, trying to get some place, and he or she misses blocking the shot by six inches or a foot, the foul happened way back there.

"On screens, you can't do that. If I let illegal contact happen, the result of that illegal contact may be four or five seconds later when the defender can't get to the guy to try and block his shot," Libbey said. "As soon as you see that early in the game, you need to pick up that illegal contact. If the defense is moving, rolling, putting up the elbow or chicken wing out or have a real wide stance … there was a situation we were looking at on film where this one player was a big guy and he would squat down when setting a pick. By squatting down, his knees opened up and caused the offense to have to go around them. That's an illegal stance. Your legs can only be as wide as your shoulders. You've got to see the whole play and you've got to make sure the guy is there."

The blind (or back) screen is set outside the field of vision of the defender. As such, the opponent must be allowed one normal step backward without contact. If contact occurs during that step or is initiated by the screener, it is a foul on the screener every time. You must judge the severity of the contact, but if it's enough to put the defender at a disadvantage, call the foul.

"On the back screen we have to make sure they're giving them the step on the back screen and we do not see enough of those plays," **Shaw** said. "We have way too many back screens set at the free throw line area that we don't call, that they run up to them or run back through them even, and we're not getting that. It's just like defensive play, you've got to see where the screener is, and you've got to know where that is, you can't get surprised by the contact."

If the ball screen is set to the side of the defender, then no distance is necessary. However, the screener must stop short of initiating contact with the defender.

"Do they have an effect on the play?" asked **Broderick**. "If it's a screen and it's just minimal contact and it has absolutely nothing to do with someone scoring a basket or getting to their offensive assignment, then it's a no-call. We have illegal screens set all the time. You have to hit an illegal screen before we can decide whether we're going to no-call or call it. You've got screens set outside the confines of their body with extended elbows and arms and chicken wings or legs, and you've got an opponent that goes up and around them, that's nothing."

Opponent Slams Into Screener

Play: A2 sets a screen to the side of stationary B3, who is looking in the other direction and is not aware of A2's presence. As B3 quickly starts a move to guard A1, B3 immediately bangs into A2 but tries to stop upon contact. **Ruling:** Good intentions, but B3 gets charged with a personal foul because A2 set a legal screen to the side, as opposed to behind, the opponent. Time and distance are not factors because the screen was on the side.

Back Screen

Play: A2 sets a screen four feet directly behind B3. B3 then moves backward, takes a step and runs into A2, who is dislodged and falls to the floor. Upon contact, B3 attempts to stop and change direction. **Ruling:** Since B3 tried to stop and not just run over A2, there is no foul despite the severity of the contact. The rationale behind the interpretation is A2's screen accomplished its objective by deterring B3's movement and to call a foul on B3 would constitute double jeopardy. That type of play will test your mettle, but don't unduly penalize the defense.

"As you're looking through your guys, set yourself up a little higher, so you can look over the shoulder of the ballhandler and not standing with your shoulders parallel to the sideline looking right at him," Libbey explained. "Look over his shoulder, which allows you to see the play as well as a screener running up behind the defender. If I'm looking through the ballhandler, then my peripheral vision will not pick up the screener. If I take a step back and angle my shoulders so I can see what's going on and shift my eyes so I can see this guy running up, then I can see if the illegal screen happens.

"A lot of that is positioning," Libbey said. "We get caught by surprise. When we see that guy turn and the contact happens, we go, 'Oh, ——!' We didn't see the whole play. We're feeling what that defender is feeling because we didn't see the whole play."

Time and distance are relevant and the opponent must be allowed both of those in order to avoid contact. The distance need not be more than two strides. If moving in the same direction, the opponent is responsible for contact if the screener stops or slows down.

No Contact, No Foul

Play: B3 intercepts a pass at the division line and is dribbling in for an easy bucket. However, A2 gives hot pursuit when B1 jumps in ahead of A2. As they head down the court, B1 cuts off A2 each time A2 attempts to go around. At no point is there any contact between B1 and A2. **Ruling:** Classic moving screen? Sure looks like one and you can count on team A's fans and players screaming for it. No matter how a screen is set or how it appears, as in that case, there can never be a foul unless illegal contact has occurred.

Enough Distance?

Play: As the ball is being advanced up the court, A3 gets five or six feet in front of B2, who's guarding dribbler A1. A3 continues in the same direction as B2. After a couple more steps, A3 suddenly stops. B2, who's in high drive, is unable to stop and pushes A3 aside. **Ruling:** It's imperative the whole sequence of that play has been observed or you may have to guess. Since A3 set the screen on a moving opponent properly (at least two strides in front), B2 was responsible for contact when A3 stopped. Pushing foul on B2.

POST PLAY CONTACT

PlayPic®

Once a position has been established, it is against the rules for an opponent to move him or her off that position.

BUMPING, GRINDING

Post play over the years has developed an element of power and leverage that puts pressure on the officials to balance the physical preparation of the players with actions that create an unfair advantage. Players will go to the basket with as much reckless abandon as they can get away with. More often, we see the line of tolerance drawn at anything short of someone being knocked down. The kicker is that many post players seem to accept the rough-and-tumble as part of the game. The problem is that it can get out of hand and lead to roughness that can sometimes get out of hand.

Officials must learn to recognize the various "tricks of the trade" that post players are commonly taught and deal with them to prevent roughness, whether the players accept it or not. As the NFHS and NCAA have often stressed in points of emphasis, officials have to stop calling what they think matters and start calling what is in the rulebook. And as it pertains to post play, that means penalizing several kinds of moves in which one or more players overcome the opponent's body position illegally.

"We need to do a better job with multiple defenders on post players when they go straight up and they are double- or triple-teamed," said **Broderick**. "We've got to make sure that they're not bowing their bodies. When they bow their bodies and extend their hips and their thighs, it actually looks like a bow. They take away their principal verticality down low, pinching them and those kind of things, walkouts. I think we need to do a better job with that."

Every player on the floor is entitled to a position on it. Once that position is established, it's against the rules for an opponent to move him or her off that position. Extending that concept, it also means that the only legal way to prevent a player from moving to a new position on the floor is to use legally gained body position as a barrier. Players can't use their arms and legs to extend their current body position; they can only use their speed and agility to move to a new body position. The rules are designed to favor whoever gets desired body position first. The official's job, then, is to recognize when body position is fairly gained and to penalize when opponents use contact to negate that. In a three official system, it most often falls to the lead official to pay attention to the post players because the activities happen just as much off the ball as on it.

"It's important at whatever level you're working to understand the guidelines for legal post play," said **George Toliver**, director of NBA D-League officials. "What can you do with your forearm? What can you do with one hand? Obviously there's no two hands. What can you legally do with your leg? Can you lift? Obviously not. Once you understand those rules as far as displacement concerns, there are two illegal acts that can occur. One is displacement by the defensive player in terms of pushing out, and the other is the offensive player going to and through the defensive player. It really is sort of a different version, almost a vertical version of the block charge, like guards while going to the basket, but you have the two vertical bodies where to and through really comes into play. If you consider that you're entitled to the position that you gain legally, to either take somebody out of that one way or the other is a displacement component that can lead to rough play, and it's just illegal in terms of the act itself. So the 'to and through' component, especially for the offensive player backing down, is really important. If you go to that person and then you go through their space, in terms of going to your next location, or push through, or turn to shoot, clearly through, then that's an offensive foul. If you are posted up and you get the ball and then that defensive player takes you away from that spot, then that constitutes a displacement by the defensive player."

UNDERCUTTING

When an offensive player posts up with his or her back to the rim, watch for the defensive player to cozy up behind in a direct line to the basket. If the attacker gets the ball in that situation with his or her feet planted, there are a lot of quick moves practiced to beat the defender. So the defensive player will work through the verticality of the player waiting for the ball by getting into the legs and forcing the offensive player off balance. The attacker needs a little longer to get his or her feet under him or herself before attacking the basket. That's an unfair advantage to the defender.

There also will be times when the attacker sits back on the defender to prevent from being fronted and to have a better chance to receive the ball. That is a foul, too. If the players stay vertical it alleviates a possibility of illegal action. The best thing the official can do is to use his or her voice early to get the player to stand "straight up." If that doesn't work, look for a clear instigator of the contact or think about a double foul if nobody's getting the message. Undercutting and its inevitable retaliatory move will go away in most cases once it starts adding to the foul count.

Watch for the attacker to attempt to back into the basket over the defender. Backing in consists of either a partial turn and a half step into the defender to bounce the defender backward. Or it can be with a dribble, with back to the basket, which displaces the defender backward in a series of nudges. Offensive players sometimes get away with that because the contact is at close range and doesn't involve much displacement with each bump. But don't forget that the defender is in legal guarding position and contact against the chest that displaces the defender is a charge and needs to be called. Watch the defender and get on the whistle when contact is on the torso and causes displacement.

"What we've tried to do philosophically is to penalize dislodgement," **Hyland** said. "If you push a guy hard enough that he is dislodged, that's going too far. That refers to the offense, too. A lot of times if you're an official sitting there in the lead trying to referee post play, if you don't call the first foul which in my experience is normally by the offense, quite frankly, those guys come down and they want to get on that block and they'll back you down or ward you off with their arm, they're all illegal moves which we don't call all of them, but that's where it usually starts in my opinion.

"Then you get the defense trying to push back and get him off the block, and using his knee, and trying to get around to three-quarter the guy or front him, and you naturally have this jostling which you'd never allow to occur on the perimeter,"

Hyland explained. "They're all fouls out on the perimeter; we all know that. But I think the game has come to expect some physical play on the post. We set down guidelines that you try to follow and keep some of the rough play out of the game, but some of it is bound to occur also."

HOOKING

Once post players get the ball with their back to the basket and figure out that bumping and grinding isn't working the way they hoped it would, they'll attempt to reverse around their opponent. That is so much easier to do, especially if they wrap their free arm around the back or across the hip of the defender, delaying the latter's movement long enough to get a foot on the floor for a clear step to the basket. Of course, that is a foul because they've extended their body position with their arm to prevent the movement of the opponent.

It's difficult for officials to call because that arm is often hidden by one or the other of the two bodies involved and it's tough to see. The way to catch that is to use the settling of the ball in at the low post as your signal to start collapsing along the baseline toward the lane. That way, you can be moving in behind the defender when the attacker makes the illegal move and pick up the foul.

If the move screens out the lead and the turn is toward the paint, the center official should have a better look to make the call.

REBOUNDING

Rebounding is about positioning, anticipation and effort as opposed to physical gifts. It is an attempt by any player to secure possession of the ball after a try or tap for a goal. Those factors represent the primary keys to success in officiating the wars of rebounding.

The key to officiating rebounding is your positioning. Regardless of what position you're in — lead, trail or center — you must obtain the proper angle to see between opponents and have a good look. Reward a player's positioning and hard work without penalizing superior athleticism. That means not guessing and recognizing the center or trail may have the best view of the play.

"Positioning is everything," said **Libbey**. "It doesn't matter where you're at. Open looks. Closed looks. We call it position adjustment. If the center and the trail are not trying to adjust on every play, then every play they are getting straightlined because the players are constantly moving. If one guy runs up to guard another guy, you've got to position yourself to see the open look. If a guy comes up and all of a sudden you get straightlined on a shot, you don't know if the shooter got hit on the shot because you're straightlined.

"And it doesn't mean bending over and looking. It means taking a step to the right or to the left. It's called active feet," **Libbey** said. "When I'm evaluating a game, I'm looking at the trail and the center: Are they stepping to the right or to the left. Are they coming out or looking down. If they are just standing there watching the play go around, it also tells me they are watching the ball. If the ball goes out of your primary, you've got to look off-ball. That will help you pick up all the other stuff, too. If the ball goes to the center's side and the center picks it up, as the trail I can drop down and pick up that illegal pick in the back. There are a lot of guys who are all over the floor watching the ball when things are happening right in front of them and they're not seeing it.

"Find open looks. You can't find open looks if you're standing flat-footed and don't have active feet," **Libbey** said.

In three-person mechanics, the lead has primary responsibility for strong-side rebounding. Depending on the lead's location along the endline when the shot is taken, the lead may step toward or away from the basket to get the best angle on the players. The trail helps on strong-side rebounding and the center takes weak side. In two-person mechanics, the trail covers the trail's side of the court and everything above the free-throw line on the lead's side. Different adjustments may be required depending on where players are and how the ball comes off the ring. On all rebounds, the " trail and center must step down toward the endline. It may only need to be one step, but it can be a huge difference in seeing the play more clearly.

Just as the good rebounder anticipates where the shot will come off, you can read clues and employ the same principles. Anticipate that every shot will be missed. Player reactions and tendencies can also provide insight. By studying shooters, learning how they miss, where their rebounds typically go and if the shooters follow their shots can be valuable in determining where you should go and whom to watch.

Keep your focus on the players, not the ball. If a shot is taken from your primary area, protect the shooter and then turn your attention to rebounding. When the shot goes up from a partner's area, find the rebounders and see the entire sequence. Know exactly how each player gets a rebound.

Pay special attention to rebounders near the ball as they have the most to gain by illegal tactics. During free throws, zero-in on the teammates of the shooter. If hands and arms of the players are at shoulder level or above, the player probably intends to legitimately contend for the miss. Hands held lower can be an indicator of pushing or holding.

Displacement is key in judging positioning. Boxing-out does not equate to riding-out, pushing, shoving or undercutting. Examine verticality by seeing the entire play, then you know if a player went up within his or her vertical space or if the player moved under an airborne opponent.

Players who crash the boards from the perimeter can present unique challenges. Because of the distance they cover, they explode onto the scene. Their built up momentum can result in a skillful play or reckless and hard contact. Allowing those "crashers" to go through opponents invites problems and leads to rougher play.

Players are getting proficient at fooling officials, or trying to. When a player can't get the ball, he or she may resort to faking a foul. If called, that team gets unmerited free throws or an extra possession. Make calls based on what you see and not what the players want you to see.

"I think we need to do a little bit better job with rebounding," said **Broderick**. "We're missing the low pushes in the back, which happens before the ball ever hits the rim. Everybody can get over the back after the ball hits the rim. I'm talking about the push that created space in the low back before the ball ever hit the rim to give them an advantage with good position.

"The toughest rebound coverage is to be rebounding and do good coverage with illegal activity before the ball hits the rim," **Broderick** said.

DISCREET CONTACT

PROTECT THE SHOOTER

We've all heard that phrase time and again at camps and clinics, but what does it really mean?

A shooter, especially an airborne shooter, is in a vulnerable position. Think about how sturdy a player is while on the floor versus in the air. A bump on the hip while standing with both feet on the floor may not have any impact. That same bump with both feet off the floor and arms extended in a shooting motion may cause the player to fall awkwardly. Therein lies the philosophy. If we don't "protect the shooter," players are more likely to become injured.

Defensive players often fly toward the shooter in an effort to block the shot. They also are taught to box out the shooter once the shot is in the air. Both situations can result in contact. Players are also taught to bump free throwers while boxing out in order to disrupt rhythm. And as if it weren't tough enough, flops are now common practice by airborne shooters trying to draw a foul.

TAP ON THE ELBOW

Even the slightest bump on the shooter's elbow can cause the ball to fly off course. A sneaky defender will actually push up on a shooter's elbow instead of chopping down at the ball because it is harder for officials to detect. The "chop" often gets called a foul, even if there's minimal contact because "it looks bad." Watch for elbow or forearm contact from setup to release.

NOT-SO-SOFT LANDING

A tough play for officials is a clean blocked shot followed by landing contact. Again, with defenders soaring toward shooters to block shots, often the defender will block the shot cleanly, only to land on the shooter because of the defender's momentum. We tend to no-call that play because of the clean blocked shot, however, a foul should at least be considered. Remember, if the shooter has by definition landed back on the court before the momentum contact, rule a common foul, not a shooting foul — regardless of whether the shot was blocked or not.

BOXING OUT SHOOTER

All well-coached teams box out shooters after release. The problem for officials comes into play when defenders turn to box out shooters while the shooter is still airborne and before the shooter has returned to the court.

Overzealous defenders must be called for blocking fouls when they box out airborne shooters and cause anything other than incidental contact. Why? It's a safety factor. Shooters (and shooters' coaches) don't like their legs being taken out, especially when they are likely concentrating on the rim with their follow-through. That can be a dangerous play and should be called a foul every time. That is a shooting foul if contact occurs before the shooter lands. Don't believe the old misconception that a shooting foul has to occur on a shooter's arm or hand.

BUMPING THE FREE THROWER

Good free-throw shooters are often superstitious. If the free thrower makes the first shot, the shooter will often want to stand in the exact same spot — never moving the feet after the shot is released — for the second or third free throw. Good luck? Maybe. It's kind of like finding a perfect golf swing and then trying to duplicate it again.

To disrupt that rhythm and karma, defenders are taught to "box out" the free thrower, which is OK, and back into or bump the shooter in order to force the shooter to take a step or two backward, which is a foul. That, theoretically, disrupts the shooter's concentration for subsequent shots.

That play is a particularly tough one for officials because it's usually a defender just being a pain to the shooter. Let the defender know that we are protecting the shooter on the free-throw line. If the contact is excessive, call it. In most cases, however, a stern "talk to" is warranted. Tell the defender that knocking the free thrower backward could be a foul and that all shooters - even free-throw shooters - are protected. The defender gets the message and the shooter feels a bit better because it's been addressed.

In extreme situations, you may consider mentioning the tactic to the offending team's captain or coach to ensure the contact doesn't continue. By letting it go unaddressed, bad blood can boil later because the bump is considered a "cheap" play. Don't let it start something bigger later on.

SPACEMAKER

Watch for that move when positions reverse and the attacker actually gets closer to the rim than the defender while waiting for the ball. That will happen when the defender tries to front the attacker or when two attackers switch and one moves to the blind side of the defensive post player. The only way the offensive player will get the ball in that case is on a delicate lob pass that gets over the defender but falls short of the weak-side coverage. What goes uncalled so often is the attacker placing a hand on the hip of the fronting defender and preventing that player from backing up under the pass. That move turns into an easy layup.

The stiff-arm is a foul because it restricts the motion of the defender, but it gets missed because there is seldom any movement imparted on the defender. From the official's perspective, it's a matter of forgetting the ball and watching the actions of the players to get the call right.

CONTACT/DISPLACEMENT CHECKLIST

✓ Illegal contact occurs when freedom of movement is disrupted with displacement, like handchecking, rough post play and/or illegal screens.

✓ There is a difference between NCAA men and women when it comes to displacement, especially with handchecks. NCAA women are allowed to "measure up" a ballhandler or dribbler once. It is also known as the "hot stove" touch. Any contact beyond that is a foul.

✓ Incidental contact with an opponent is permitted and does not constitute a foul. The mere fact that contact occurs does not mean a player has committed a foul.

✓ Verticality applies to legal position. A legal guarding position must be attained initially and movement thereafter must be legal. From that position, the defender may rise or jump vertically and occupy the space within his or her vertical plane.

✓ Beware of the offensive player violating the principle of verticality by "clearing out" or causing contact within the defender's vertical plane, which is a foul.

✓ Handchecking, body bumping and moving screens are all types of perimeter contact that are illegal by the offense and defense.

✓ Bumping, undercutting, hooking and positioning between players going for rebounds are all areas that officials must recognize and determine illegal contact or displacement.

✓ Officials need to watch for discreet forms of contact/displacement created by defenders, including a bump on the shooter's elbow, fouling a shooter after a blocked shot, boxing out the shooter or free-throw shooter overzealously.

FINAL WORD ON TOUGHEST CALLS

TRAVELING

"I think we've made progress in traveling because I think we are talking about it a lot more. Traveling, to me, is a play that you cannot defend, so you have to remove indefensible, illegal plays from the game, otherwise how can you defend them? If you let the low post player travel off a drop step, you can't defend him."

— John Adams

"You set the table as far as what you're going to put up with that night early in the game. We all wish that everybody was consistent and on the same page and called everything according to the rules the way they should. I think consistency is important for the game, like getting walks early. You need to get the first walk, but you need to get almost every walk. The initial move by a player in possession of the ball is key to traveling. You've got to know where the pivot foot is and what you can do with the pivot foot."

— Tom Lopes

"When I was coaching 25 years ago, every time a female player head faked, they would call a travel and it wasn't. There's been a consistent theme for a long time in the women's game that they can make some legal moves that may not look like the men, but you have to determine first if they are they legal, and if they are legal, don't penalize it. Don't call a travel just because it looks unusual."

— Debbie Williamson

BLOCK/CHARGE

"We need to know when the defense established legal guarding position. Two feet down and facing and if we have an airborne player. It's not easy. There are a lot of factors. Then you have the rules side of it depending what rule code you are in. If you are officiating men's collegiate, you can't be under the basket. If you're officiating women's collegiate or high school, you can be. It's about refereeing the defense."

— Mary Struckhoff

"The contact doesn't have to be dead center in the defensive player's chest to be a player control foul, it's the entire frame of the body when the defensive player is in his or her legal guarding position."

— Roger Barr

"There's a myth where they say, 'Oh, they were still moving.' Well, if you establish legal guarding position you can move. You can move to protect yourself, you can move backwards to retreat and keep a legal defensive stance or defend your opponent. I always get a kick out of it when they say, they're still moving."

— Patty Broderick

"In the NBA, both feet do not have to be on the floor like they do in college or high school. When we talk about a player having to beat the (dribbler) to a spot, we're talking about the torso. The other thing with the NBA with block/charge is the defender has to be there once I start the upward shooting motion. Once I start that motion, the defender cannot slide anymore. He has to be there. The continuous shooting motion starts once I gather the ball. Once I gather and on my next step, you hit me, it's a two-shot foul."

— Joe Borgia

CONTACT/DISPLACEMENT

"We go on the premise of rhythm, speed, balance and quickness — R-S-B-Q. If any of those factors occur while the offense has the ball, like the defense knocking the ballhandler off his rhythm or knocking him off his speed, balance or quickness, then that's a foul."

— Dave Libbey

"If the defense does nothing wrong, then the only thing you can have is either an offensive foul or a play on. I think too many times the defense is legal, but because of the contact and because of the reactions of the players after the contact, we're calling defensive fouls. I really stress that you have to know where the defensive player was from the start of the play until the time the contact occurs. If he's done nothing wrong within that sequence, you can never have a defensive foul."

— Curtis Shaw

"It's important at whatever level you're working to understand the guidelines for legal post play. What can you do with your forearm? What can you do with one hand? Obviously there's no two hands. What can you legally do with your leg? Can you lift? Obviously not. Once you understand those rules as far as displacement concerns, there are two illegal acts that can occur: One is displacement by the defensive player in terms of pushing out and the other is determining if the offensive player is going to and through the defensive player."

— George Toliver

"We have to teach our officials, and the better officials are better at this, to understand that there's going to be some contact, and secondly, there's going to be some really good blocked shots out there. Players are allowed to block a shot, and there's going to be some contact, and if they're vertical, they shouldn't be penalized for it."

— John Lozano

"Everybody would love to have continuity in a game. Usually when the ball is going in the basket you have a great game, it's relatively easy to referee, and people go off saying, that was a great game to watch. But what happens if you have a team with 10 or 11 players that love to foul and they don't think that you're going to call all the handchecks? So you call all the handchecks and now all of a sudden you're interrupting the game. But the official is doing his job. You're supposed to call them all. But the game is interrupted all the time, no one likes it, but has the official done a bad job or has he done his job correctly? From my standpoint we're trying to change the way the team plays. You're not allowed to handcheck every time down the court. Change your ways because that's a disadvantage to one team if you're allowed to handcheck. It's not so much a disadvantage if you only call two or three a game when you're actually fouling 12 or 15 times a game."

— Art Hyland

FINAL WORD

REFEREE *magazine*
Is **Better** than ever

▶ **12 ISSUES OF *REFEREE* MAGAZINE FOR JUST**

$29.95

Every issue is packed with the latest officiating news, up-to-date rules information and interpretations, special features on relevant issues like training, industry hot topics, and interviews with the top personalities in officiating.

In each issue of *Referee*:

- Journal of Record Reports
- In-depth Articles and Features
- Rules, Mechanics and Techniques
- Caseplays
- Interviews
- *NEW* **All Sports** section – containing game management, philosophies, tips and techniques that apply to <u>all sports</u>.

Don't delay – **Save 64%** off the cover price and get the next 12 issues for only $29.95*!

Name _____

Address _____

City _____ State _____ Zip _____

Email _____

Please check one of the following boxes:

☐ Renewal ☐ New Subscriber ☐ Payment Enclosed ☐ Bill Me Later

Send to: 2017 Lathrop Ave.
　　　　　Racine, WI 53405

▶ Go to **www.referee.com/promo/P05SUBR** or call **1-818-487-4549**

Please make sure to mention Promotion code: **P05SUBR** when ordering.

*U.S. Only